C000282743

MIDDLESBROUGH FC

MISCELLANY

MIDDLESBROUGH FC

MISCELLANY

TONY MATTHEWS

FOREWORD BY DAVID MILLS

AMBERLEY

This book is dedicated to all the players who,

over the years, have represented Middlesbrough football club

through thick and thin.

First published 2014

Amberley Publishing
The Hill, Stroud
Gloucestershire, GL5 4EP

www.amberley-books.com

Copyright © Tony Matthews, 2014

The right of Tony Matthews to be identified as the Author
of this work has been asserted in accordance with the
Copyrights, Designs and Patents Act 1988.

All rights reserved. No part of this book may be reprinted
or reproduced or utilised in any form or by any electronic,
mechanical or other means, now known or hereafter invented,
including photocopying and recording, or in any information
storage or retrieval system, without the permission in writing
from the Publishers.

British Library Cataloguing in Publication Data.
A catalogue record for this book is available from the British Library.

ISBN 978 1 4456 4154 6 (print)
ISBN 978 1 4456 4168 3 (ebook)

Typesetting Amberley Publishing.
Printed in the UK.

FOREWORD

Middlesbrough Football Club has a rich, proud and distinguished history. Founded in 1876, it has long been at the very heart of the community, despite having rivals Newcastle United and Sunderland as neighbours.

Over the course of time, the club has been served by a host of great players. In the early years, it was Steve Bloomer, followed by George Elliott and George Camsell. The former helped 'Boro finish third in the top flight in 1913/14 – their highest-ever League placing – while Camsell starred in 'Boro promotion-winning teams as Second Division champions in three seasons. In 1926/27, he netted a staggering 59 League goals and 1928/29 struck another 30. He was some player.

In the late 1930s, 'Boro claimed seventh, fifth and fourth places in quick succession in the top flight, giving everyone a run for their money!

After the Second World War, when England internationals George Hardwick, Micky Fenton and Wilf Mannion were in full flow, the team at times was a force to be reckoned with. After that came Brian Clough, who was another wonderful goal-scoring centre-forward.

In the mid- to late fifties and early 1960s, many more star players donned the famous red-and-white strip, among them Gordon Jones, Bill Harris, Alan Peacock, Eddie Holliday, Arthur Kaye, Ray Yeoman and Bill Gates. These were followed by the likes of John Hickton (alongside whom I played many times), Frank Spraggon, Stuart Boam, Eric McMordie, Willie Maddren, John Craggs, goalkeeper Jim Platt and Tony McAndrew. There were many more, all of them great club men, totally committed out on the field of play.

I must say I had the pleasure of playing in a great team in the mid-1970s under manager Jack Charlton. We won the Second Division title in a canter in 1973/74, reached the quarter-finals of the FA Cup in each of the following three seasons, the third time under boss John Neal, and we even won the Anglo-Italian Cup. The backing from the fans at Ayresome Park was superb.

Moving forward into the 1980s, and many more exceptionally fine players served the club, including 'Mr Consistency' David Armstrong, David Hodgson, goalscorer Bernie Slaven and top defender Tony Mowbray, who later returned to the club as manager.

Promoted again in 1991/92, 'Boro were founder members of the Premiership the following season. Although relegation was suffered immediately, the team bounced back in 1995, only to slip back down again in 1997 when 'Boro reached the FA Cup final for the very first time, losing to Chelsea. They also lost in successive League Cup finals 1997 and 1998.

'Boro played Premiership football once more from 1998 to 2009, during which time they won their first major trophy, lifting the League Cup in 2004. This earned them a place in the UEFA Cup, the final of which they reached in 2005/06. And over the last twenty-two years, since the Premier League started, 'Boro have certainly been blessed with many more talented footballers, the Brazilian Juninho and Italian striker Fabrizio Ravanelli among them.

Being a dedicated 'Boro-ite' myself, and having had the pleasure and, indeed, the honour to have been associated with the club as a player and coach, I have always appreciated how important football is to the fans. To many, it is the single most important thing in life outside their family. Hundreds, perhaps thousands, simply live and breathe their local team and the players. Indeed, everything connected with the name Middlesbrough is in their blood.

And why not?

The *Middlesbrough FC Miscellany* contains everything you need to know about this great club. There's so much information, including a lot of things I never knew happened. It's simply a great read.

On that note, I must congratulate author Tony Matthews, a friend of mine from my West Brom days, along with his researchers, assistants and, indeed, the publishers for compiling such a magnificent book.

Read it, enjoy it – this is another splendid acquisition to add to your Middlesbrough collection.

David Mills
(Middlesbrough player 1967–79, 1984–86; coach 1986/87, 2008/09)

INTRODUCTION

This book is an easy-to-read mini encyclopedia of Middlesbrough Football Club.

Since the day the club was first formed, in 1875/76, headlines have been made: some for good reasons, some for bad. Initially, 'Boro played non-League football, taking on the likes of Tees Wanderers, Tyneside Association, South Bank and their arch-rivals at that time, Redcar.

After winning the FA Amateur Cup in 1895 and 1898, 'Boro gained a place in the Second Division of the Football League, finishing in fourteenth place in its first season. In 1901/02, the team achieved promotion to the First Division, where 'Boro would stay for the next eighteen League seasons.

Between 1924 and 1929, they went down twice and gained promotion twice before having a second eighteen-year run in the top flight. Between 1954 and 1966, the home fans at Ayresome Park watched Second Division football and in 1966/67, for the first time in the club's history, 'Boro competed in the old Third Division – a place they revisited in 1986/87 after short spells in Divisions One and Two.

Prior to joining the Premiership in 1992, 'Boro gained promotion in successive seasons. The club has spent fifteen of the last twenty-two years in the top flight and the other seven in the Football League Championship (second tier), but will be aiming to reclaim their Premier League status in the not too distant future ... this season perhaps!

Over the course of time, more than 700 players have donned the club's red-and-white strip, and some thirty managers have taken charge of the team. And everyone has always given their all, no matter what the circumstances. Obviously, some players never fit in; similarly, a manager failed to bring success. But nevertheless, they all tried, and over the course of time others will follow both on the pitch and off it.

I have tried to cram everything into this pocket-sized almanac, and I'm sure you will find it exceptionally interesting. Read about the great players, 'Boro's big wins, heavy defeats, the club's Wembley triumph and disappointments, champion goalscorers, record appearance-makers, the men who have led Town through thick and thin, and lots, lots more.

This book is for all Middlesbrough supporters, young and old, male and female, to enjoy.

Tony Matthews, 2014

ACKNOWLEDGEMENTS

I would like to say a special thank you to Tom Furby of Amberley Publishing for agreeing to produce and publish this book – my 128th on football since 1975, and my first on Middlesbrough FC.

I must also thank ex-'Boro player David Mills, supporter Terry Jackson (a friend of mine here in Spain and a fan of George Hardwick); my loving and long-suffering wife Margaret, who once again has had to withstand the noise of my fingers tip-tapping away on the computer keyboard; and the dedicated staff at Amberley Publishing who have made this book look quite superb.

NOTES ON TEXT

Where a single year appears in the text (when referring to an individual player's career or club record) this indicates, in most cases, the second half of a season: i.e. for 1975 read 1974/75. However, when the figures (dates) appear thus: 1975–80, this means seasons 1975/76 to 1979/80 inclusive and not 1974–75 to 1980–81.

If you spot any discrepancies, errors and omissions, or would like to add anything to the text in this book, I would appreciate it greatly. You can contact me (via the publisher) so that all can be amended in any future publications regarding Middlesbrough Football Club. With the advantage of the internet, several extra facts and figures relating to 'Boro FC and its players have been found that had not previously been known or made public.

MIDDLESBROUGH FC

MISCELLANY

BIRTH OF THE CLUB

It is now known that Middlesbrough Football Club was formed at a meeting of several local cricket club members at the gymnasium inside the Albert Park Hotel on 20 October 1876. John Greenwood was named as secretary-treasurer and he quickly signed up a decent squad of players. Middlesbrough FC was up and running.

FIRST GAMES

It is on record that Middlesbrough FC played its first game early in 1877. It lasted just 40 minutes (20 minutes each way) and was billed as a 'home friendly' against the local rugby team, Tees Wanderers. It ended in a 1-1 draw. Later that year, on 22 December 1877, 'Boro played their first competitive away game, losing 1-0 to Barnard Castle. Three weeks later, they won their first match, beating South Bank 4-0 at home, before drawing with a strong Tyne Association XI in Albert Park, in front of around 150 spectators.

TEAM HONOURS

Middlesbrough have won quite a few prizes over the years and here is a list of honours achieved by the club since its first runners-up prize (in the Northern League) in 1890/91:

Football League Second Division / Football League Division One
Champions 1926/27, 1928/29, 1973/74, 1994/95
Runners-up 1901/02, 1991/92, 1997/98

Lootball League Third Division
Runners-up 1966/67, 1986/87

Northern League
Champions 1893/94, 1894/95, 1896/97
Runners-up 1890/91, 1891/92, 1897/98

Football League
Winners 2004
Runners-up 1997, 1998

FA Cup
Runners-up 1997

UEFA Cup
Runners-up 2006

Anglo-Scottish Cup
Winners 1976

FA Amateur Cup
Winners 1895, 1898

Zenith Data System Cup
Runners-up 1990

FA Youth Cup
Winners 2004
Runners-up 1990, 2003

Kirin Cup
Winners 1980

CLUB LEGENDS

These are the ten players – 'Legends of Middlesbrough' – voted for by the fans as part of a campaign with the *Evening Standard*:

Player	Seasons	Apps	Goals
George Camsell	1925–39	453	345
George Hardwick	1937–50	166	7
Wilf Mannion	1936–54	368	110
Brian Clough	1955–61	222	204
John Hickton	1966–77	499	187
Willie Maddren	1968–77	354	21
Tony Mowbray	1982–2000	425	29
Bernie Slaven	1985–93	381	146
Juninho*	1995–2004	155	34
Gareth Southgate	2001–07	204	4

*Had three spells with 'Boro: 1995/96, 1999/2000 and 2002/04.
All appearances (including those made as a substitute) and goals scored appertain to all competitions (friendlies/tours not included).

HALL OF FAME

Eleven men, who either played for or managed Middlesbrough during their respective careers, are featured in the English Hall of Fame. They are (A–Z order): Malcolm Allison, Viv Anderson, Steve Bloomer, Jack Charlton, Brian Clough, Paul Gascoigne, Wilf Mannion, Bryan Robson, Graeme Souness, 'Nobby' Stiles and Terry Venables.

THREE CUP FINALS, ONE VICTORY

Middlesbrough reached the final of the Football League Cup in 1997, 1998, and 2004. They lost the first two but were triumphant at the third attempt, beating Bolton Wanderers at Wembley.

On the way to the final in 1996/97, 'Boro beat Hereford United 10-0 on aggregate (7-0 at home, 3-0 away) in round two, eased past Huddersfield Town 5-1 in round three, saw off Newcastle United 3-1 in round four and edged out Liverpool 2-1 in round five, all at home, before beating Stockport County 2-1 on aggregate (2-0 away and 0-1 at home) in the two-legged semi-final. The final against Leicester City at Wembley, in front of 76,757 spectators, ended level at 1-1 (after extra-time) only for 'Boro's hearts to be broken when Steve Claridge netted a 100th minute winner in the replay at Hillsborough before 39,428 fans.

The very next season, en route to the final with Chelsea, 'Boro knocked out Barnet 3-0 on aggregate (with 2-0 and 1-0 victories), Sunderland 2-0 at home, Bolton Wanderers 2-1, also at home (but after extra-time when Craig Hignett struck the winning goal in the 115th minute), Reading 1-0 away with another dramatic late goal from Hignett, and Liverpool 3-2 on aggregate in the semi-final, losing 1-2 at Anfield before running out 2-0 victors at Ayresome Park, both goals coming inside the first four minutes.

The final, which took place in front of 77,698 fans at Wembley, went to extra time when Chelsea netted twice through Frank Sinclair and Roberto Di Matteo to win the game 2-0.

'Boro's run to the final in 2004 started with a hard-fought 1-0 extra-time home win over Brighton & Hove Albion, following up with 2-1 victory at Wigan in round four. Their next two games both resulted in 5-4 penalty shoot-out victories, the first over Everton at Goodison Park after a 0-0 draw, and the second against Tottenham Hotspur, following a 1-1 draw after 120 minutes of all-out action at White Hart Lane.

A crowd of 72,634 turned out for the Wembley final, which saw 'Boro get off to a flying start, Job and Zenden scoring inside the first seven minutes. Davies pulled one back for Bolton halfway through the first-half, but 'Boro's battling defence held firm and a delighted Gareth Southgate went up to collect the club's first-ever major trophy … after 120 years of trying!

PARK THRILLER

The first Football League game with a 7-5 result took place on 13 February 1915, when Middlesbrough beat Tottenham Hotspur in a Division One game at Ayresome Park watched by 7,500 spectators. Walter Tinsley scored a hat-trick for 'Boro, while Jimmy Cantrell netted four times for Spurs. Earlier in the season, the teams had played out a 3-3 draw at White Hart Lane. Eighteen goals in two matches – that's great value for money.

OPPOSING MARKSMEN

Thierry Henry loved playing against Middlesbrough! The Arsenal striker scored 12 goals in 14 appearances against 'Boro. Alan Shearer (Blackburn/Newcastle) netted 10 in 18 games, while W. G. Richardson (West Bromwich Albion) bagged 9 in 9.

STOPPER TO TEACHER

Andy Dibble, who made 23 appearances for 'Boro in two spells with the club in the 1990s, and almost 400 during his nomadic career, became a fine goalkeeping coach, firstly with Accrington Stanley (June 2005–November 2006), Coventry City (November 2006–March 2007), Peterborough United (March 2007–May 2009) and Rotherham United (since July 2009).

FIRST CUP GAME

Middlesbrough competed in a Cup tie for the first time in 1879, when they took on and lost to Sheffield Exchange in the Sheffield Cup at Linthorpe Road in front of some 1,000 spectators.

GOGO – GOSH!

As a youngster, Middlesbrough forward Bryan Orritt played for the club with the longest name in football: Llanfairpwllgwyngyllgogerychwyrndrobwllllantysiliogogogoch. The Welsh club's fifty-eight-word name was shortened to Llanfair PG, and Orritt, born in Caernarfon, played there in 1952/53 before signing for Bangor City. He moved to Birmingham City in 1956, switched to 'Boro in 1962 and ended his career in South Africa with Johannesburg Rangers. Orritt died in 2014, aged seventy-seven.

RELEASED BY LIVERPOOL

Craig Hignett was a youth team player with Liverpool for two seasons (1986–88), but was allowed to leave Anfield by manager Kenny Dalglish without making the first team. Over the next 19 seasons, up to 2006/07, the Merseyside-born striker scored 168 goals in 566 senior League and Cup appearances while serving with twelve different clubs. He bagged 48 goals in 195 outings for Middlesbrough between 1992 and 1998 and 57 in 165 games for Crewe Alexandra in two spells. Hignett also had a trial with Leeds United.

PADDY POWER

Over the course of time, there has been a strong Irish link with Middlesbrough FC, with several players appearing for the club at senior level. These include:

Bob Braithwaite (Belfast), Wes Bryne (Dublin), Brian Close (Belfast), Terry Cochrane (Killyleagh), Johnny Crossan (Derry), Michael Cummings (Dublin), Peter Desmond (Cork), Arthur Fitzsimons (Dublin), Willo Flood (Dublin), Connor Gallagher (Derry), Jason Gavin (Dublin), Jimmy Hartnett (Dublin), Chris Johnson (Dublin), Graham Kavanagh (Dublin), Pat Lynch (Belfast), Jim McCabe (Derry), Eric McManus (Limavady), 'Eric' McMordie (Belfast), Alex

McNeill (Belfast), Joe Miller (Belfast), Alan Moore (Dublin), Frank Mulholland (Belfast), Joe Murphy (Belfast), Olly Norris (Derry), Charlie O'Hagan (Buncrana), Keith O'Halloran (Dublin), Keith O'Neill (Dublin), Don O'Riordon (Dublin), Jim Platt (Ballymoney), Martin Russell (Dublin) and Bert Smith (Donegal). Curtis Fleming was born in Manchester, Chris Morris in Newquay, Cornwall, Andy Townsend in Maidstone, Kent and Bernie Slaven in Paisley, Scotland, yet all four played for the Republic of Ireland.

Fleming gained ten caps (all with 'Boro), Morris won thirty-five overall (his last with 'Boro in 1993), while Townsend collected no less than seventy during his career, four of which came as a 'Boro player.

Alan Kernaghan, born in Otley, Yorkshire, was capped by Northern Ireland as a schoolboy and went on to win a total of twenty-two full caps for the Republic of Ireland, the first seven with 'Boro.

Also as 'Boro players, Braithwaite won seven caps, Cochrane (19), Crossan (1), McMordie (21), Miller (3) and Platt (20) for Northern Ireland in full internationals while Desmond (4), Fitzsimons (25), Hartnett (2), Moore (8), O'Neill (2) and Slaven (7) played for the Republic of Ireland during the respective careers with Middlesbrough.

And don't forget Jack Charlton, who managed Middlesbrough between 1973 and 1977, was also boss of the Republic of Ireland national team (1986–96).

HAT-TRICK HEROES

Jackson Ewbank is credited with having scored Middlesbrough's first hat-trick, doing so in a 3-1 replay win over Redcar in front of 2,500 spectators in a Sheffield Cup tie in October 1880.

Joe Murphy scored a hat-trick on his debut for 'Boro, in an 8-1 home league win over Burton Swifts in November 1899. And Italian superstar Fabrizio Ravanelli also netted three times in his first game for 'Boro, in a thrilling 3-3 home Premiership draw with Liverpool in August 1996.

GOALS GALORE

Between them, Steve Bloomer and George Camsell scored a total of 407 goals for Middlesbrough in League and FA Cup competitions. Bloomer's contribution was 62 in 130 appearances while Camsell bagged a staggering 345 goals in 453 outings. These two wonderful marksmen both had excellent careers in top-class football.

Bloomer, who was born in Cradley Heath, deep in the heart of the Black Country, in January 1874, and played for both West Bromwich Albion and Wolverhampton Wanderers, netted a grand total of 422 goals in 678 competitive club and international matches between 1892 and 1914 while playing for Derby County (two spells), Middlesbrough and England, for whom he won twenty-three caps. He died in Derby in April 1938, aged sixty-four.

Camsell was born in Framwellgate Moor, County Durham in November 1902 and played League and FA Cup football for Durham City and Middlesbrough for fifteen years from 1924 to 1939. In that time, he scored a total of 383 goals in 483 football matches for Durham City, Middlesbrough and England (nine caps won). Camsell died in Middlesbrough in March 1966.

Together the combined records of Messrs Bloomer and Camsell is quite staggering: 805 goals scored in 1,161 games. Camsell also netted 21 times in 33 regional games for Middlesbrough during the Second World War.

CLOSE CALL

Middlesbrough needed a single point from their last two League games of the 1952/53 season to escape relegation from the First Division. They needn't have worried as they won them both, beating Manchester United 5-0 at home and Portsmouth 4-1 away. In fact, 'Boro looked dead and buried with eight games remaining. But following a 2-0 home win over the League champions-elect for that season, Arsenal, they won four and drew two of their last seven fixtures to climb up to a respectable thirteenth.

WORLD TOURIST

Between 1993 and 2007, Hamilton Ricard played League football for clubs in nine different countries: Colombia (with Deportivo Cali, Independiente Santa Fe and Cortulua), Bulgaria (CSKA Sofia), England (Middlesbrough), Japan (Shonan Bellmare), Ecuador (Emelec), Cyprus (Apoel), Spain (Numancia), Uruguay (Danubio) and China (Shanghai Shenhua). A Colombian international, capped twenty-seven times, Ricard scored 106 goals in a total of 324 appearances for his eleven clubs.

BENEFIT CHIEF

The first player to receive three benefits with different clubs was outside-right Tommy Urwin. His first was with Middlesbrough in 1921/22, and thereafter with Newcastle United and Sunderland. He retired in 1935 with 445 League and FA Cup appearances under his belt, 200 for 'Boro (14 goals scored), 200 for the Magpies (24 goals) and 55 for the Wearsiders (6 goals).

ONE-GOAL WONDERS

In the 1914/15 League season, Middlesbrough scored once in each of sixteen First Division matches, including a sequence whereby they netted one goal in eight games on the run between mid-October and early December. In fact, they scored once in fourteen games out of a possible nineteen during the first half of the season.

FIRST £1,000 PLAYER...

The first four-figure transfer fee in English football saw centre-forward Alf Common move from Sunderland to Middlesbrough for £1,000 in February 1905. After the deal was completed, 'Boro were denounced for 'buying' their way out of the relegation and the transfer-fee limit was quickly enforced. Common scored 4 goals in 10 games at the end of that 1904/05 season, helping 'Boro rise to fifteenth in the table. He subsequently left Ayresome Park for Woolwich Arsenal in August 1910 for just £100, one-tenth of his original fee.

...AND THE £500,000 MAN

In January 1979, utility forward David Mills became the first half-a-million-pound footballer to move from one English club to another. He was signed by Ron Atkinson, joining West Brom for £516,000.

THE CHOSEN FEW

Five Middlesbrough players lined up in the Cleveland representative side that beat Northumberland & Durham 10-0 in February 1881. This friendly was arranged to celebrate the newly formed Cleveland FA.

ATTENDANCES (HIGH AND LOW)

Since joining the Football League in 1899, Middlesbrough's home attendance record has been broken sixteen times. This is the official breakdown:

10,000	v. Small Heath	FL2	9 September 1899
11,000	v. Lincoln City	FL2	1 September 1900
12,000	v. Glossop	FL2	15 September 1900
13,000	v. Small Heath	FL2	15 December 1900
16,000	v. Newcastle United	FAC	9 February 1901
24,769	v. West B. Albion	FAC	23 March 1901
30,000	v. Sunderland	FL1	12 September 1903
33,400	v. Manchester City	FAC	9 March 1904

35,703	v. Sunderland	FL1	6 November 1920
38,067	v. Sheffield United	FL1	3 February 1923
43,754	v. Manchester City	FL 1	27 December 1926
45,854	v. Sunderland	FL1	1 January 1938
46,747	v. Arsenal	FL1	12 March 1938
51,080	v. Sunderland	FAC	21 January 1939
51,612	v. Bolton Wanderers	FAC	13 February 1946
53,802*	v. Newcastle United	FL1	27 December 1949

*Some references give this attendance as 53,536

The eight lowest crowds to watch Middlesbrough play a home game (various competitions) have been:

700	v. Grimsby Town	WW2	14 December 1940
1,000	v. Darlington	WW2	16 December 1939
1,000	v. Doncaster Rovers	WW2	7 December 1940
1,000	v. Bradford City	WW2	11 January 1941
1,633	v. Brescia Calico	AIC	22 December 1993
2,177	v. Carlisle United	FMC	8 October 1985
2,500	v. Luton Town	FL2	21 October 1899
2,985	v. Ancona	AIC	16 November 1993

ATTENDANCE FACTS

1. Middlesbrough's lowest home crowd for an FA Cup tie was just 1,000 versus Staveley in November 1883, and the lowest for a League Cup matchwas 3,915 v. Northampton Town in September 2001.

2. Away from home, the lowest audiences Middlesbrough have played before have all been in the Anglo-Italian Cup competition: 300 v. Udinese in October 1994; 500 v. Pisa in October 1993; 996 v. Grimsby Town in August 1993; and 1,200 v. Ascoli in November 1993.

3. The biggest away crowd to watch Middlesbrough in a Premier League game was 75,967 against Manchester United at Old Trafford in April 2007.

4. Prior to the introduction of the Premiership (League) in 1992, and not including Cup finals, 'Boro's biggest 'away' League crowd was 65,279 at Manchester United in September 1946 (Division One). In the FA Cup it has been 63,418, also at Manchester United in February 1970, and in the League Cup, the biggest was also away to Manchester United, 49,501 in December 1974.

5. The attendances at Middlesbrough's five Wembley Cup finals were: 76,369 (*v.* Chelsea, ZDSC in 1990), 76,757 (*v.* Leicester City, LC in 1997), 79,160 (*v.* Chelsea, FA Cup, also in 1997), 77,698 (*v.* Chelsea, LC, 1998) and 72,634 (*v.* Bolton Wanderers, LC, 2004).

6. The lowest crowd at Middlesbrough League Cup tie (anywhere) was 2,356 away at Hartlepool United in August 1986.

7. Middlesbrough's best average home League attendance for a single season was 36,123 from 21 games in 1950/51 (Division One). The club's best away average was 38,630, set twice, in 1948/49 (also in Division One) and in 1950/51.

8. The club's lowest average home League crowd wass 5,135 in 1984/85 (Division Two). Prior to that, the lowest had been 5,271 in 1899/1900 (also in Division Two) while the 1985/86 average was 6,257 (again in Division Two).

9. The unusual crowd of 7,777 attended the Colchester United *v.* Middlesbrough second round League Cup tie at Layer Road in September 1965.

10. A record crowd of 27,599 saw Middlesbrough beat Carlisle United 2-1 in a fifth-round FA Cup tie in February 1970 at Brunton Park.

11. Prior to 1925, the attendance figure at a Football League game was usually given in round figures: i.e. 10,000, 20,000, 30,000, etc.

12. The largest crowd to watch a Middlesbrough game in their single season of First World War football was 20,000 at home to Sunderland in March 1919 (lost 1-2) and the biggest during the seven seasons of Regional Second World War football was 32,211 against Newcastle United at St James' Park in September 1945 (drew 1-1).

VOID FIXTURES

Middlesbrough, like all other clubs, played three Football League games at the start of the ill-fated 1939/40 season before the competition was abandoned due to the outbreak of the Second World War. These are details of 'Boro's three First Division matches:

26 August 1939	*v.* Aston Villa (a) 0-2	Attendance 32,427
30 August 1939	*v.* Liverpool (a) 1-4*	Attendance 16,762
2 September 1939	*v.* Stoke City (h) 2-2	Attendance 12,298

*Micky Fenton scored all three 'Boro goals, And these fixtures were subsequently declared null and void by the Football League.

FIRST CAP, FIRST GOAL

Ben Lewis was the first Middlesbrough player to win a full international cap when he starred for Wales against Scotland in 1893. Bob Atherton was the first 'Boro player to score an international goal, doing so for Wales against Scotland in 1904.

'I WILL RETURN' (AND THEY DID)

Several players have had two (sometimes three) spells with Middlesbrough. Here are a few who returned to the club (loan deals included) during their respective careers: David Hodgson (1978, 1987), Juninho (1995, 1999, 2002), Tony McAndrew (1973, 1984), John McNally (1895, 1898), David Mills (1968, 1974), Jaime Moreno (1994, 1997), Gary Pallister (1984, 1998), Stephen Pears (1983, 1985), Mark Proctor (1978, 1989), James Stott (1891, 1899), James Suddick (1896, 1902), Gary Walsh (1995, 2000), Andrew Wilson (1914, 1921), Jonathan Woodgate (2006, 2012) and 'Bolo' Zenden (2003, 2004).

Others came back to the club as a manager having initially worn the red and white as a player, and they are Willie Maddren and Tony Mowbray. Harold Shepherdson was a player who returned to Ayresome Park as assistant trainer (1948) and then head trainer.

REAL 'BORO

I believe that four players have served with both Middlesbrough and Real Madrid. They are Cameroon international midfielder Geremi (with 'Boro in 2002/03), French sweeper Karembeu (2000/01), Spanish goalkeeper Tomas Mejias (signed on loan in 2014) and central defender Jonathan Woodgate (three spells, starting in 1993). And we can't forget Aitor Karanka, who was assistant coach at the Bernabeu before taking over from Tony Mowbray as 'Boro's manager in November 2013.

FIRSTS AT AYRESOME PARK

A crowd of 7,000 saw the first goal scored at Ayresome Park by Willie White in Middlesbrough's 1-0 friendly win over Celtic on Saturday 5 September 1903. Around 30,000 then saw the first League goal on the ground, which arrived four days later when 'Boro's captain Joe Cassidy netted in the forty-first minute of what turned out to be a 3-2 defeat at the hands of Wearside rivals Sunderland.

BARCELONA CONNECTION

According to my research, four players have been associated with both Barcelona and Middlesbrough. They are Spanish full-back Gaizka Mendieta (signed by 'Boro in 2003), Dutch defender Michael Reiziger (2004/05), Brazilian midfielder Fabio Rochemback (2005/06) and Reiziger's fellow countryman, 'Bolo' Zenden (2004/05). Sir Bobby Robson, a Middlesbrough amateur in 1948, managed Barcelona in 1996/97.

SEQUENCES

Here are details of Middlesbrough's record-breaking sequences in the Football League (various divisions):

Wins in succession: 9 (16 February 1974–6 April 1974)
Most defeats in a row: 8 (26 December 1995–17 February 1996)
Most draws on the trot: 8 (3 April 1971–1 May 1971)
Unbeaten run: 24 (8 September 1973–19 January 1974)
Without a League win: 19 (3 October 1981–6 March 1982)
Best scoring run: 26 (21 September 1946–8 March 1947)
Non-scoring run: 5 (17 January 2009–21 February 2009)
NB: In their five goalless games in 2009, 'Boro failed to find the net against West Bromwich Albion (0-3), Chelsea (0-2), Blackburn Rovers (0-0), Manchester City (0-1), and Wigan Athletic (0-0)

STILL TO PLAY

Middlesbrough have yet to play these eleven current Football League clubs in a senior competition, as of 2014/15: AFC Wimbledon (new club formed in 2002), Cheltenham Town, Crawley Town, Exeter City, Fleetwood Town, Morecambe and Stevenage.

SENT DOWN BY ARCH RIVALS

Middlesbrough's final League game of the 1927/28 season was against arch-rivals Sunderland at Ayresome Park. At the time, both clubs were deep in trouble at the bottom end of the First Division table and 'Boro knew that a draw would be good enough to secure their top-flight status. A crowd of almost 42,000 turned up for this vital encounter, including 10,000 from Wearside. And it was the visitors who celebrated by whipping 'Boro 3-0 with goals by Jimmy Mathieson (on 13 minutes), David Halliday (55) and John Smith's own goal late on. For the record, never before had a team suffered relegation from the First Division with as many points as 'Boro achieved in 1927/28 (37). The 1921 FA Cup winners Tottenham Hotspur were demoted with 'Boro.

PROMOTED AT THE FIRST ATTEMPT

On 4 May 1929, exactly a year after being relegated, Middlesbrough regained their First Division place by beating Grimsby Town 3-0 at Ayresome Park in front of 36,503 spectators. George Camsell netted twice and outside-left Owen Williams once as 'Boro claimed the Second Division title. Ex-Middlesbrough manager Wilf Gillow was in charge of the Mariners.

OPEN DAY

Over 21,000 people, old and young, male and female, attended the first official Open Day at Middlesbrough's Ayresome Park ground on 26 July 1981. Those who turned up were allowed to visit the dressing room, directors' suite, boardroom and press room, and have a good look at what goes on behind the scenes at the club.

FIRST FROM SCOTLAND

The first team from north of the border to play Middlesbrough was Govan, who travelled down from Scotland to contest a friendly match on 8 January 1877 at Linthorpe Road. 'Boro's Jack Sammerson guested for the visitors, who were beaten 3-1 by 'Boro in front of 1,000 hardy spectators.

ON YOUR BIKE!

Middlesbrough left-half, and boyhood supporter, David Murphy, a big pal of Wilf Mannion, loved football. He made 15 first-class appearances for the club before the outbreak of the Second World War. So keen was he to play during the early part of the 1940s, that one day, after missing the bus from Redcar, he was forced to travel by train to Middlesbrough. Arriving late, he borrowed a stranger's bicycle and pedalled his way to the ground, shattered but determined to line up with his teammates. A dedicated footballer, Murphy sadly lost his life on a French battlefield in September 1944, at the age of just twenty-seven.

NO RETURN TICKET

Middlesbrough's South African-born goalkeeper Arthur Lightening was given permission by the club to return to his home country to attend his brother's wedding in May 1963. He never returned to Ayresome Park. He made 18 appearances for 'Boro.

FIVE ON TELEVISION

The television cameras were present at Middlesbrough's third-round FA Cup tie away at Swansea in January 1981 and in front of 18,015 fans at the Vetch Field, and millions more watching their screens, the team in red rose to the occasion by whipping their Welsh opponents 5-0. David Hodgson (2), Billy Ashcroft, Michael Angus and Terry Cochrane scored the goals to earn 'Boro a home tie with West Bromwich Albion in the next round.

FIRST MASCOT

Young Andrew Gaun became Middlesbrough's first 'official' mascot when he led the team out ahead of their final home League game of the 1967/68 season against Bristol City. A crowd of 12,684 saw 'Boro win 2-1, both goals being scored by centre-forward Stan Webb.

UEFA CUP DISAPPOINTMENT

After battling through fourteen matches in the 2005/06 UEFA Cup competition, Middlesbrough unfortunately crashed to a 4-0 defeat at against Spanish club Sevilla in the final in front of 31,000 spectators in Eindhoven, Holland. This was 'Boro's run through to the final:

First round, first leg	Skoda Xanthi	(h) 2-0	Attendance 14,191
First round, second leg	Skoda Xanthi	(a) 0-0	Attendance 5,013
Group D	Grasshoppers	(a) 1-0	Attendance 8,500
	Dnepr	(h) 3-0	Attendance12,953
	AZ Alkmaar	(a) 0-0	Attendance 8,461
	Litets	(h) 2-0	Attendance. 9,436
Third round, first leg	VfB Stuttgart	(a) 2-1	Attendance 21,000
Third round, second leg	VfB Stuttgart	(h) 0-1	Attendance 24,018
Fourth round, first leg	AS Roma	(h) 1-0	Attendance 25,354
Fourth round, second leg	AS Roma	(a) 1-2	Attendance 32,642
Fifth round, first leg	FC Basel	(a) 0-2	Attendance 23,639
Fifth round, second leg	FC Basel	(h) 4-1	Attendance 24,521
Semi-final, first leg	Steaua Bucharest	(a) 0-1	Attendance 22,000
Semi-final, second leg	Steaua Bucharest	(h) 4-2	Attendance 34,622
Final	Sevilla	(n) 0-4	Attendance 30,988

Middlesbrough's line-up in the final was Mark Schwarzer, Stuart Parnaby, Franck Queudrue (sub. Ayegbeni Yakubu), George Boateng, Chris Riggott, Gareth Southgate, James Morrison (sub. Massimo Maccarone), Fabio Rochemback, Jimmy Floyd Hasselbaink, Mark Viduka (sub. Lee Cattermole) and Stewart Downing. Viduka top-scored with six goals, Maccarone netted five, Hasselbaink four, Yakubu two (one penalty) and Boateng, Parnaby and Riggott all one each. In the final, 'Boro were 1-0 down after 26 minutes and pressing for an equaliser when Enzo Maresca (ex-West Bromwich Albion) scored twice for Sevilla in the 78th and 84th minutes; the fourth goal came right at the death.

HOT-SHOT BROWN

Centre-forward Alex 'Sandy' Brown scored a record 15 goals in the FA Cup for Tottenham Hotspur in the 1900/01 season, including all 4 in the semi-final victory over West Bromwich Albion. One of the game's best headers, Brown, a Scottish international, finished up as Middlesbrough's leading scorer in his first season with the club, hitting 17 goals in 1903/04. He netted on his debut against Sheffield Wednesday and was on target in the first-ever game played at Ayresome Park (*v.* Sunderland).

GASCOIGNE: AWAY FROM FOOTBALL

In 1998, Paul Gascoigne first entered sustained therapy sessions when he was admitted into Priory Hospital after a drinking session in which he drank thirty-two shots of whisky, which left him at rock bottom. 'Boro manager Bryan Robson then signed him into the clinic while the former England international was unconscious. He was released, at his own request and insistence, two weeks into the suggested minimum stay of twenty-eight days. His subsequent visits to the same hospital became more infrequent, and he eventually lapsed back to alcoholism. In 2001, Gascoigne's then Everton chairman Bill Kenwright contacted the player's therapist at the Priory, John McKeown, who organised more treatment to help the midfielder to control his drinking. As part of the treatment, he was sent to the USA, where he was registered into a clinic in Cottonwood, Arizona. There he was diagnosed with bipolar disorder and had a stay at the clinic. Following on, after suffering low points when working in China, and again in 2004 after retiring from football, he returned to Cottonwood for more treatment.

The year 2004 saw the publication of Gascoigne's autobiography, *Gazza: My Story*, written with Hunter Davies. In the book, and also in his later title, *Being Gazza: Tackling My Demons,* published in 2006, he refers to treatment for bulimia, obsessive-compulsive disorder (OCD), bipolar disorder and alcoholism.

The two books also describe in detail his addictive personality, which has led him to develop addictions of varying severity to alcohol, chain smoking, gambling, high-caffeine energy drinks, exercise and junk food.

In February 2008, Gascoigne was sectioned under the Mental Health Act after a possible suicide attempt at the Malmaison Hotel in Newcastle-upon-Tyne. He was taken into protective custody by the local police to prevent self-harm.

On 9 July 2010, Gascoigne appeared at the scene of the tense stand-off between the police and Raoul Moat, claiming to be a friend of Moat and stating that he had brought him a can of lager, some chicken, a fishing rod, a Newcastle shirt and a dressing gown. He was denied access to Moat, who was wanted at the time for shooting three people. Moat subsequently killed himself after a police stand-off.

In August 2011, Gascoigne sued *The Sun*, claiming its coverage of the Raoul Moat incident interrupted his treatment for alcoholism.

On 20 October 2010, he admitted being more than four times over the limit at Newcastle-upon-Tyne Magistrates' Court. He should have appeared in court to be sentenced for drunk driving, but instead he went into rehab on the South Coast of England. As a result, and in his absence, Gascoigne was given an eight-week suspended sentence.

In 2013, his agent, Terry Baker, informed BBC Radio 5 Live that his man, Gascoigne, had relapsed again: 'He won't thank me for saying it but he immediately needs to get help ... His life is always in danger because he is an alcoholic. Maybe no one can save him – I don't know. I really don't know.'

Gascoigne was placed in intensive care in a US hospital while being treated for alcoholism in Arizona in a rehabilitation programme, thanks to financial support provided by ex-cricketer Ronnie Irani and television presenter and radio DJ Chris Evans.

In January 2014, Gascoigne entered rehab for his alcohol addiction for a seventh time at a £6,000-a-month clinic in Southampton.

THE YOUNG ONES

The average age of Middlesbrough's team at the start of their Premiership game against Fulham on 7 May 2006 was just twenty. The line-up was: Turnbull (21), Bates (19), Davies (21), Taylor (19), Wheater (19), Cattermole (18), Johnson (18), Kennedy (19), Morrison (19), Christie (the old man of the pack at 27) and Graham (20). On the bench were Cooper (aged 39), Walker (17) and Craddock (19).

£17 BILL

In May 1938, Brentford transferred right-half Duncan McKenzie to Middlesbrough and as a gesture the player's removal bill from London to the North East of England amounted to £17, which was covered by his new club, 'Boro. McKenzie paid some of that fee back by scoring once (in a 3-2 home win over Leicester City) in twenty-eight League appearances before the Second World War interrupted his career.

GOLDEN OLDIES

Bryan Robson, at the age of thirty-nine years, eleven months and twenty-one days, is the oldest player ever to appear for Middlesbrough in a first-class match, doing so against Arsenal at the Emirates Stadium on 1 January 1997. Robson beat goalkeeper

'Tiny' Williamson's record of thirty-eight years and nine months, which he set seventy-four years earlier, in March 1923.

Danny Coyne, aged thirty-eight years, five months and two days, is 'Boro's oldest FA Cup player. He appeared *v.* Coventry City, away, on 29 January 2012, when 'Boro lost 3-1.

Gareth Southgate was thirty-five years, eight months and seven days old when he starred against Sevilla in the 4-0 UEFA Cup final defeat in Eindhoven on 10 May 2006.

Viv Anderson, aged thirty-eight years and 215 days, became Middlesbrough's oldest debutant when he lined up for the club against West Bromwich Albion in a League game on 1 April 1995. Ten players aged thirty-five and over have appeared in first-class matches for Middlesbrough.

It is believed that Willie Fernie is the oldest former Middlesbrough player alive today. He will be eighty-six in November (born in 1928). Ex 'Boro goalkeeper Rolando Ugolini was eighty-nine years of age when he died in April 2014.

Wilf Mannion played his last game of football in 1980 at the age of sixty-two, turning out for Earlstown, a local village team in Newton-le-Willows, near St Helens.

AYE AYE SKIPPER

To some people, it is a privilege to captain your team and over the years, scores of players have led out the 'Boro team in various League and Cup matches over the years. Here are a select few: Bob Atherton, Bob Baxter, Billy Birrell, Stuart Boam, Joe Cassidy, Lee Cattermole, Colin Cooper, Paul Ince, Tony McAndrew, Peter McCracken, Tony Mowbray, Jack Peacock, Bryan Robson, Gareth Southgate, Bob Stuart and Bob Watson. Southgate was 'Boro's skipper for the 2006 UEFA Cup final against Sevilla.

JACK'S 'LITTLE GEM'

David 'Spike' Armstrong, Jack Charlton's 'Little Gem' when he was manager of Middlesbrough, was only twenty-five years old when the club granted him a testimonial in 1980. Armstrong, who served the club from 1972 to 1981, made 431 appearances for 'Boro, gained a Second Division championship medal in 1974, won the club's Player of the Year award in 1979/80, played for England against Australia at the end of that season (the first of three full caps) and when he moved to Southampton in 1981 it was for a record fee of £600,000.

AND THE YOUNGSTERS

Luke Williams, aged sixteen years, six months and seventeen days, is the youngest player to line up for Middlesbrough at senior level, doing so against Barnsley in a Championship game on 28 December 2009.

Bryan Morris, aged sixteen years, eight months and 10 days, is the club's youngest FA Cup player appearing *v.* Hastings United at home on 5 January 2013.

Andy Campbell, aged sixteen years, eleven months and seventeen days, is 'Boro's youngest Premiership player *v.* Sheffield Wednesday, also at home, on 5 April 1996.

Adam Johnson, aged seventeen years, eight months and thirty-three days, starred in the UEFA Cup against Sporting Lisbon in Portugal on 17 March 2005.

Another youngster to play for 'Boro was Stephen Bell, who made his first appearance for the club in January 1982, at home to Southampton (Division One) at the age of sixteen years, ten months and eighteen days.

Full-back Alan Wright, who played for 'Boro in 2003, made his League debut as a sixteen-year-old for Blackpool against Chesterfield in May 1988.

HOT-SHOT ALVES

Afonso Alves scored a hat-trick in Middlesbrough's 8-1 home Premiership win over Manchester City on 11 May 2008. This was the second game in which he had played that season when 9 goals were scored. Seven months earlier, on 7 October 2007, he had netted three times for his previous club, SC Heerenveen, in a 9-0 Dutch League victory over Heracles.

THEY DIED TOO YOUNG

Three of Middlesbrough's Scottish-born players – centre-half Andrew Jackson, full-back Don McLeod and outside-right Archie Wilson – all lost their lives during the First World War. Jackson (aged twenty-three, with 123 appearances to his name) died in France in 1918; McLeod (aged thirty-five, with 135 appearances to his credit) was killed in Belgium in 1917 and Wilson (aged twenty-six, with just 23 games under his belt), also perished in France in 1916. Left-half David Murphy, from South Bank, was killed in action when serving in the Middle East in September 1944. He was just twenty-seven years of age.

Apart from the four players mentioned above, several other footballers who were associated with Middlesbrough sadly passed away far too young, among them:

Stephen Bell	Born 1965, died 2001, aged thirty-six
Neville Chapman	Born 1941, died 1993, aged fifty-two
Len Goodson	Born 1880, died 1922, aged forty-two
Willie Hamilton	Born 1938, died 1976, aged thirty-eight
Joe Harris	Born 1896, died 1933, aged thirty-seven
Bob Hume	Born 1941, died 1997, aged fifty-six
Bosco Jankovic	Born 1951, died 1993, aged forty-two
'Paddy' Johnson	Born 1924, died 1971, aged forty-seven
Cyril Knowles	Born 1944, died 1991, aged forty-six
Sam Lawrie	Born 1934, died 1979, aged forty-four
Willie Maddren	Born 1951, died 2000, aged forty-nine
Andrew Ramsay	Born 1877, died 1908, aged thirty-one

| Jim Stott | Born 1871, died 1908, aged thirty-seven |
| Ken Thomson | Born 1930, died 1969, aged thirty-nine |

*Thomson died of a heart attack on Castle Eden golf course.

PITCH TO PUB

Several footballers, at various levels, choose to move into the pub/licensing trade after retiring. Here are a few ex-Boro players who chose to pull pints in later life:

Andrew Aitken (Tyneside), Billy Ashcroft (Merseyside), Harry Bell (became an executive with Tetley Brewery), Bill Bilcliff (Ferryhill), Billy Brawn (Brentford, London), John Brown (North Ormesby), George Carr (North Ormesby), Alf Common (Darlington), Alan Foggon (Teeside), Billy Forrest (Billingham hotelier), Tom Griffiths (Wrexham), Harry Leonard (Derby), Alf Maitland (North Shields), Don Masson (Nottingham hotelier), Dick Neal (Penkridge, Staffs), Robert Page (Middlesbrough), Billy Pease (North East), Fred Priest (Hartlepool), Charlie Scrimshaw (Stoke-on-Trent), Jim Stott (Newcastle), Mark Summerbell (North East), Johnny Vincent (Birmingham, Oldbury), Russell Wainscoat (Humberside), Jim Watson (Shildon) and Charlie Wayman (worked for the Scottish & Newcastle brewery). Former 'Boro manager Alex Mackie became licensee of the Garter Hotel, Middlesbrough.

CAP THAT!

Wilf Mannion holds the record for winning the most full international caps as a Middlesbrough player. He appeared in 26 senior games for England (11 goals scored) between September 1946 and October 1951. Mannion also played in four Second World War internationals collected two 'B' caps, played for the Football League side on seven occasions and starred in three miscellaneous representative matches.

As a 'Boro player between 1949 and 1958, Arthur Fitzsimons was capped 25 times by the Republic of Ireland. Terry Cochrane (1978–82), Jim Platt (1976–83) and Eric McMordie (1968–72) won 19, 20 and 21 caps respectively for Northern Ireland as 'Boro players during the years stated; John Mahoney collected 13 for Wales (1977–79) and Jock Marshall and Andy Wilson each won six caps for Scotland in the 1920s.

'BORO AND ENGLAND

Around sixty players who appeared at senior level for Middlesbrough also represented England in full internationals, and there have also been others who guested for the club during the Second World War. More stars became 'Boro managers and/or coaches, and some were on the club's books as youngsters but never made the first team.

Here is a list of 'Boro's 'England internationals' as at 2014:

John Alderson, Stan Anderson, Viv Anderson, David Armstrong, Phil Bach, Mark Barham, Nick Barmby, Kevin Beattie, Ralph Birkett, Steve Bloomer, Billy Brawn, Arthur Brown, George Camsell, Jacky Carr, Brian Clough, Alf Common, Colin Cooper, Terry Cooper, Arthur Cunliffe, Brian Deane, Stewart Downing, Ugo Ehiogu, George Elliott, Micky Fenton, Paul Gascoigne, George Hardwick, Eddie Holliday, Paul Ince, Andy Johnson, Cyril Knowles, Mick McNeil, Wilf Mannion, Brian Marwood, Paul Merson, Danny Mills, Jackie Mordue, Tom Morren, Gary Pallister, Ray Parlour, Alan Peacock, Joe Peacock, Billy Pease, Fred Pentland, Fred Priest, Stan Rickaby, Bryan Robson, Michael Ricketts, Arthur Rigby, Stuart Ripley, Bill Scott, Nobby Stiles, David Thomas, Michael Thomas, Tommy Urwin, Russell Wainscoat, Maurice Webster, 'Tim' Williamson, Owen Williams, Jimmy Windridge, Jonathan Woodgate and Luke Young.

Second World War international guests were Walter Boyes, Allenby Chilton, Bobby McNeal, Bill Nicholson and Jackie Robinson; two amateurs who went on to win full cap were Bobby Robson and Chris Smalling. Those who assisted 'Boro in other capacities include four managers: Raich Carter, 1966 World Cup winner Jack Charlton, David Jack and Terry Venables; four coaches: Steve Howey, Brian Little, David Nish and Colin Todd, while Mick Mills was engaged as a 'Boro scout.

CENTURIAN

At 2014, only twenty-five footballers had scored 100 or more goals in the Premiership, and one of them played for Middlesbrough – Jimmy Floyd Hasselbaink. The Suriname-born forward, who was with 'Boro from 2004 to 2006, netted a total of 127 goals during his career, which also saw him serve with Leeds United, Chelsea and Charlton Athletic.

NORTH AMERICAN STARS

Here is an unofficial list of players who have been associated with Middlesbrough during their respective careers, and have also served with clubs in the USA/Canada Leagues:

Ian Bailey (Minnesota Kicks), Branco (New York/New Jersey MetroStars), Peter Brine (Minnesota Kicks), David Chadwick and Terry Cochrane (both with Dallas Tornadoes), Stan Cummins (Minnesota Kicks), Terry Garbutt (New York Cosmos), Ray Hankin (Vancouver Whitecaps), John Hickton (Fort Lauderdale Strikers), John Honeyman (J & P Coates/Rhode Island), Kei Kamara (Orange County Blue Star, Columbus Crew, San Jose Earthquakes, Houston Dynamo, Sporting Kansas City), Ray Lugg (Fort Lauderdale Strikers), Carlos Marinelli (Kansas City Wizards), Jack Marshall (Belmont FC/New York, Brooklyn Wanderers, Bethlehem Steel), Don Masson (Minnesota Kicks), Tony McAndrew (Vancouver Whitecaps), Jaime Moreno (DC Washington MetroStars), Don O'Riordon (Tulsa Roughnecks), Frank Spraggon (Minnesota Kicks), David Thomas (Vancouver Whitecaps), Alan Willey (Minnesota Kicks) and Abel Xavier (LA Galaxy).

Also, John McCormack emigrated to Canada and played for Canadian Select XI; ex-Boro player Nobby Stiles managed Vancouver Whitecaps; and 'Boro amateur Sir Bobby Robson was player-manager of the Vancouver Royals.

HAT-TRICK SPECIALISTS

George Camsell scored a club record twenty-four hat-tricks for Middlesbrough; he also bagged two five-timers and netted four goals in a game on nine occasions. Brian Clough weighed in with seventeen hat-tricks, one five-timer and five four-goal hauls; George Elliott struck thirteen trebles for 'Boro plus one four-timer; Micky Fenton claimed ten hat-tricks and two four-timers; Alan Peacock registered three goals in a game on seven occasions and a four-timer twice; Bernie Slaven popped in seven hat-tricks and Andy Wilson delivered three trebles and one five-timer.

Three players scored hat-tricks in Middlesbrough's 9-3 home FA Cup win over Goole Town in January 1915. They were Jacky Carr, George Elliott and Walter Tinsley.

RECORD GOALSCORERS

This is how Middlesbrough's seasonal goalscoring record has been set and broken (and/or equalled) and by whom, since the club entered the Football League in 1899:

Season	Player	League Goals	League/Cup
1899/1900	Charlie Pugh	7	7
1900/01	Bill Wardrope	11	14
1901/02	Jack Brearley	22	23
1912/13	George Elliott	22	25
1913/14	George Elliott	31	31
1919/20	George Elliott	31	34
1921/22	George Elliott	32	32

| 1925/26 | Jimmy McClelland | 32 | 38 |
| 1926/27 | George Camsell | 59 | 63 |

CONSECUTIVE APPEARANCES

David Armstrong never missed a game for Middlesbrough in eight years (1972–80). During that time, he made a total of 358 consecutive appearances for the club, a record that will probably never be beaten!

Top Eight Consecutive League Appearances

305	David Armstrong	1972–80
190	Ray Yeoman	1958–63
136	Bernie Slaven	1985–88
130	'Tiny' Williamson	1907–11
129	Bill Harris	1954–57
125	Willie Maddren	1972–76
121	Tony Mowbray	1985–88
105	Stuart Boam	1972–75

Top Five Consecutive Appearances in All Matches

358	Armstrong	149	Maddren
207	Yeoman	142	Mowbray
159	Slaven		

CAREER APPEARANCES

Listed here are some of the players who starred for Middlesbrough who had exceptionally fine careers overall, making over 600 League appearances at senior level.

Bryan Robson	674	Brian Deane	630
Peter Beagrie	670	Paul Merson	621
John Wark	651	Colin Cooper	606
Chris Kamara	642	Steve Bloomer	600
Dean Windass	639		

Steve Bloomer's total includes one Test match appearance for Derby County against Notts County in April 1895, and he was also the first player in the history of the game to make 600 Football League appearances, reaching this milestone on 24 January 1914, when he lined up for Derby against Bradford City at Valley Parade. Three other 'Boro managers (after Robson) all topped the 600 mark in League appearances: Colin Todd (649), Gordon Strachan (638) and Jack Charlton (628).

DISGRACED

Brian Phillips, centre-half with 'Boro (1954–60), was suspended from competitive football in 1962, and later banned for life and jailed for his part in a bribery racket. Phillips admitted 'offering a bribe' to Middlesbrough's goalkeeper Esmond Million while he was a player with Mansfield Town.

Hamilton Ricard was sentenced to three months in jail for dangerous driving in 2007. The Columbian played for 'Boro the four years, from March 1998 until March 2002, when he was transferred to CSKA Sofia in Bulgaria.

Ken Thomson ('Boro centre-half for three seasons from 1959 to 1962) was suspended sine die by the Football League for 'illegal activities', having become ensnared by police in an alleged bribery probe.

PLAYER, DIRECTOR, CHAIRMAN

Phil Bach was born in Ludlow, Shropshire in September 1872 and moved north to Middlesbrough as a child. A competent right-back, he signed for 'Boro, then an amateur club, at the age of sixteen in 1888 and stayed for seven years, playing in only a handful of FA Cup games for 'Boro. In 1895, he moved south to Reading and returned to the North East in 1897 to sign for Sunderland.

In February 1899, Bach made his only international appearance for England against Ireland, which ended in a 13-2 victory for England.

The 13 goals scored by England remains a record to this day and Bach had a hand in three of them. In April 1899, Bach rejoined 'Boro, but failed to break into the first team and subsequently switched to Bristol City, later assisting Cheltenham Town. After retiring he developed hotel interests in Gloucestershire and later Middlesbrough.

He became a director of 'Boro in February 1911 and six months later was appointed chairman in place of the disgraced Thomas Gibson-Poole. Bach was asked to 'rebuild the club' following the match-fixing scandal involving Gibson-Poole and manager Andy Walker.

He appointed Tom McIntosh as the team's new manager. Bach served as chairman until 1925, and had a second spell in the 'chair' from 1931 to 1935. He later served on the FA Council for twelve years, until his death in 1937, and was on the international selection committee from October 1929. Also on the Football League Management Committee and President of the North Eastern League, Bach was a key member of the FA for a number of years before his death in 1937 at the age of sixty-five.

COLOURFUL BUNCH

Forward David Black (1890s); ten players named Brown – 'Sandy' (1903), Arthur (1912), goalkeeper David (1977), Jim (1900), Jock (also 1900), ex-apprentice jockey John (1906), Joe (1946), Tom (1920), Tom E. (1953) and Billy (1928); plus Alan White (1994), Willie White (1903) and Derek Whyte (1992) have all been 'colourful' footballers with Middlesbrough in first-class competitions.

NAMED JOB

Here is a list of certain Middlesbrough players whose name could mean they had another job, even a title: Steve Baker, Michael Barron, Marlon King, David Knight, Alan Miller, Joe Miller, Lee Miller and Dan Nurse.

PLAY-OFF GLORY

At the end of the 1987/88 season, Middlesbrough beat Bradford City 3-2 on aggregate in the two-legged Division Two play-off semi-final before overcoming top-flight Chelsea 2-1 in the first-ever two-legged play-off final. It also meant that Chelsea were the first team to be relegated from Division One via the play-offs, while at the same time 'Boro, who had finished third in Division Two, became the first club to gain promotion via this same system. Bruce Rioch was the 'Boro manager at the time.

PENALTY STOPPER

Mark Crossley, who played for Middlesbrough between 2000 and 2003, is one of only two goalkeepers (Dave Beasant is the other) to save a penalty in an FA Cup final in normal playing time, doing so for Nottingham Forest against Tottenham Hotspur (taken by Gary Lineker) at Wembley in 1999. Crossley is also the only 'keeper to save a League penalty taken by Matt Le Tissier, playing for Nottingham Forest against Southampton in March 1993. Crossley himself also scored a goal for Sheffield Wednesday against Southampton in December 2006. His dramatic late strike, from a corner, earned the Owls a point from a 3-3 draw.

ENGLAND AT AYRESOME PARK

There were three full internationals staged at Ayresome Park, the details of which are:

25 February 1905	England 1 Ireland 1	Attendance 21,700
14 February 1914	England 0 Ireland 3	Attendance 25,000
17 March 1937	England 2 Wales 1	Attendance 30,608

Two Middlesbrough players figured on the score sheet in the 1905 game: Steve Bloomer for England and Tim Williamson, with an own goal, for the Irish. 'Boro's centre-forward George Elliott played for England in the 1914 encounter, and Stan Matthews scored a rare goal in the 1937 victory over Wales.

ON TRIAL

An international trial took place at Ayresome Park in February 1928 when an England XI beat the Rest of the World 8-3 in front of 18,000 spectators. Everton's 'Dixie' Dean scored five of England's goals. 'Boro stars Jacky Carr (England) and George Camsell (The Rest) opposed each other and Camsell netted once for his side.

SIX-ALL

On 22 October 1960, Charlton Athletic drew 6-6 with Middlesbrough at The Valley. 'Boro trailed 1-0 and then led 2-1, 4-3 and 6-4 before the Addicks netted twice late on to salvage a point. Seven of the twelve goals were scored in a seventeen-minute spell before the interval when the teams went in level at 4-4. Brian Clough ('Boro) and Dennis Edwards (Charlton) both bagged hat-tricks in front of 10,604 spectators. This result equalled the highest scoring draw in Football League history, Leicester City having shared twelve goals with Arsenal in a First Division game in April 1930.

GOAL MACHINES

Only ten players have scored over 100 goals in first-class matches for Middlesbrough. They are:

George Camsell	1925–39	345
George Elliott	1909–25	213
Brian Clough	1955–61	204
John Hickton	1966–77	187
Micky Fenton	1932–50	162
Bernie Slaven	1985–92	146
Alan Peacock	1955–64	141
David Mills	1969–85	111
Wilf Mannion	1936–54	110
Billy Pease	1926–33	102

Camsell was Middlesbrough's leading scorer ten seasons running, from 1926/27 to 1935/36. He was second best in 1936/37 and jointly in 1937/38 (see *100 Goal Man,* page 45). Elliott finished up as top marksman seven times between 1910/11 and 1922/23, and was second-highest scorer on three occasions in 1914/15, 1923/24 and 1924/25. He also holds the club record for most goals scored in any game (11) for 'Boro's second XI in a 14-1 win over Houghton Rovers in 1909/10. Hickton also topped 'Boro's goalscoring list on seven occasions; Slaven was top dog six times; Fenton and Clough both headed the charts on five occasions; Mills three times; Peacock twice and Mannion once (1952/53). Elliott was the First Division leading scorer in 1913/14 with 31 goals; Camsell headed the Second Division charts in 1926/27 with a total of 63 (59 in the League).

In League football alone, Camsell, with 325 goals, is the club's champion marksman; Elliott netted 203, Clough 197, Hickton 159, Fenton 147, Peacock 125, Slaven 118, Mannion 99 and Pease also scored 99. Camsell also scored a record 20 FA Cup goals for 'Boro; Fenton netted 15 and Hickton 13. Hickton also holds the record for most League Cup goals for the club: 13.

Local man Clough joined Middlesbrough as an amateur in November 1951, turned professional in May 1952 and remained at Ayresome Park until July 1961, when he signed for neighbours Sunderland. Making his League debut in September 1955, over the next six years or so, as a hot-shot centre-forward, he averaged almost a goal a game, scoring 204 times in 222 competitive games. He also netted 27 times in friendlies and once in an abandoned game as well as hitting five goals for the Football League representative side against the Irish League in 1959, making it 237 goals in six years.

Slaven found the net for 'Boro in seven different competitions: Football League (118), FA Cup (4), League Cup (10), Play-offs (2), Full Members Cup (1), Simod Cup (2) and Zenith Data Systems Cup (9). He also found the net in friendly matches and for the 'Boro's second XI.

100-GOAL MAN

George Camsell scored exactly 104 competitive goals in two seasons for Middlesbrough (1926/27 and 1927/28). The centre-forward netted 92 in the League and 8 in the FA Cup, and he also notched another 5 in two tour games in Denmark in May 1927. Only Steve Bull has equalled this feat in the history of the game. He scored 102 goals in two seasons for Wolves (1987/88 and 1988/89).

SPORTING PRISONER OF WAR

After retiring as a player, Steve Bloomer went to Germany in July 1914 to coach Britannia Berlin '92. However, within three weeks of arriving in the country, the First World War broke out and he found himself interned at Ruhleben, a civilian detention camp in the Spandau district of Berlin.

Bloomer was one of several former professional footballers among the detainees. Others included his former England colleagues Fred Spiksley and Sam Wolstenholme; his former Middlesbrough colleague Fred Pentland; Scottish international John Cameron; John Brearley, once of Everton and Tottenham Hotspur; and a German international, Ed Dutton, who had previously played for Britannia Berlin 92. The camp contained up to 5,500 prisoners. Gradually, a mini-society evolved and football became a popular activity. The Ruhleben Football Association was formed and Cup and League competitions were organised, with as many as 1,000 attending the 'big' games. The teams adopted the names of established teams and in November 1914, Bloomer captained a Tottenham Hotspur XI, which included the aforementioned Dutton, to victory in the annual

Cup Final against an Oldham Athletic XI. The game was refereed by Everton player Wolstenholme.

On 2 May 1915, an England XI, featuring Pentland, Wolstenholme, Brearley and Bloomer, played a World XI captained by Cameron. Bloomer also played cricket at the camp and in May 1915 a Ruhleben XI, featuring himself and Brearley, played a Varsities XI in the Ruhleben Cricket League. In July 1916, a Lancashire XI, featuring Bloomer, beat a Yorkshire XI that included Wolstenholme. In summer, several sports-minded prisoners turned to the game of cricket, which was played on The Oval in front of large crowds. Bloomer established the camp batting record with one spectacular swash-buckling innings of 204 and he also recorded bowling figures of 6 for 15. Athletics events were also arranged and Bloomer won the 'Old Age Handicap' at the Ruhleben Olympics, covering the 75 yards in 9.6 seconds. Everybody in camp knew 'Steve' 'Paleface' Bloomer,and when he finally left Ruhleben in March 1918, a farewell football match was staged in his honour.

Between October 1923 and April 1925, Bloomer was coach to the Real Union club.

BLOOMIN' PEST!

Steve Bloomer scored 422 goals in 678 club and international matches. He netted 332 in 525 games in two spells for Derby County (1892–1906 and 1910–14), bagged 62 in 130 outings for Middlesbrough (1906–10) and claimed 28 in 23 full internationals for England.

SUPER SUBS

Slovakian forward Szilárd Németh holds the record for the most substitute appearances for Middlesbrough. Of his 146 first-class appearances, accumulated between 2001 and 2006, no less than 65 were made by coming off the bench (55 in the League). Alan Kernaghan (53), Phil Stamp (52), Robbie Mustoe (43), Stuart

Ripley (43), Italian Massimo Maccarone (41), James Morrison (38), Frenchman Joseph-Désiré Job (37), Andrew Campbell (36) and Craig Hignett (36) make up the top ten.

SOO WHO!

Wing-half Frank Soo was the first player of Chinese descent to appear in a Football League game. He made his debut for Stoke City against Middlesbrough on 4 November 1933 at Ayresome Park and was on the losing side by 6-1.

LOSING 1-0

The first time a scoreboard was used at a Football League ground to indicate half-time scores of other matches was at Linthorpe Road, Middlesbrough, on Saturday 6 September 1902, when Everton were the visitors for a Division One match.

PLAYER-BOSS

The first player-manager to appear in a League Division One game was ex-Newcastle United centre-half Andy Aitken, who starred for Middlesbrough against Liverpool on 3 November 1906. He had officially joined 'Boro for £500 just three days earlier.

GREAT SEASON

Under manager Jack Charlton, Middlesbrough stormed to the Second Division title in 1973/74, creating some very impressive stats in the process. This was their full record:

Venue	P	W	D	L	F	A	Pts
Home	21	16	4	1	40	8	36
Away	21	11	7	3	37	22	29
Total	42	27	11	4	77	30	65

'Boro won the Championship by 15 points from second-placed Luton Town; thirteen different players featured on the score-sheet: Alan Foggon was leading marksman with 19 League goals, while Stuart Boam and David Armstrong were both ever-present. 'Boro's biggest win was 8-0 at home to Sheffield Wednesday, and their heaviest defeat was 5-1 at Nottingham Forest. Goalkeeper Jim Platt kept 24 clean-sheets in 40 appearances. The average League attendance at Ayresome Park was 22,498 (the best since 1959/60); the biggest crowd was 37,030 *v.* Sunderland, the lowest 14,742 *v.* Aston Villa. Away from home, the best gate was 41,658 at Sunderland, the lowest just 6,958 at Swindon.

CLUB CREST

The official Middlesbrough crest has gone through four changes since the club's formation. Initially, the badge on a player's shirt was simply the crest of the town with a red lion instead of a blue lion in order to fit in with the club's colours. Following the adoption of the white band on the shirts in 1973, only the red lion remained with the letters 'M.F.C.' underneath in red. This was further adapted following the reformation of the club in 1986 to a circular crest with the lion in the middle and the words 'Middlesbrough Football Club 1986' around the circle in order to reflect this new era. In 2007, the club changed its crest once again, this time featuring a lion inside a shield and the words 'Middlesbrough Football Club 1876' underneath. The club stated that this was to reflect the club's long history and not just their post-liquidation status.

NOMADIC FOOTBALLERS

Dean Gordon, who made 71 appearances for Middlesbrough between 1998 and 2001, played for twenty different football clubs between 1990 and 2014. His other nineteen were, in turn, Crystal Palace (his first before 'Boro), Cardiff City, Coventry City, Reading, Grimsby Town, Apoel Nicosia, Crook Town (2 spells), Blackpool, Lewes (2 spells), Worksop, Albany United, Auckland City, New Zealand Knights, Torquay United, Whitby Town, Ilkeston Town, Glapwell, Workington and Thornaby.

Utility forward Alex McMulloch, who appeared for 'Boro in the season 1907/08, served with eighteen different football clubs between 1903 and 1922. His other seventeen were non-League sides Bonnyrigg Rose, Leith Athletic, Broxburn United and Edinburgh St Bernard's in Scotland; Newcastle United, Bradford Park Avenue, Brentford, Swindon Town (two spells), Reading, Coventry City, Raith Rovers, Alloa Athletic, Dunfermline Athletic, Heart of Midlothian, Lincoln City, Merthyr Tydfil and finally Llanelli in Wales.

Andy Dibble served with sixteen different clubs as a player (1982–2005) and three as a goalkeeping coach (up to 2014). He also played for Wales and was with Middlesbrough in the 1990s.

Striker Marcus Bent scored 97 goals in exactly 500 League appearances while assisting fifteen clubs between 1995 and 2003. His employers were, in turn: Brentford, Crystal Palace, Port Vale, Sheffield United, Blackburn Rovers, Ipswich Town, Leicester City, Everton, Charlton Athletic, Wigan Athletic, Birmingham City, Middlesbrough, Queens Park Rangers, Wolverhampton Wanderers, Sheffield United (again) and Mitra Kukar (Indonesia).

JOB LOT

It is always interesting to learn what other jobs footballers took up after retiring from the game. Here are a few of the odd (and no-so-odd) jobs that players chose to do after taking off their boots. Some are still in their new job today:

Mick Angus	Served in the local police force.
Bob Appleby	Cumberland-based water bailiff.

David Armstrong	Soft drinks salesman in Southampton.
Billy Ashcroft	Recorded a pop 'song' when playing in Holland.
Harry Blackmore	Butcher in Exeter, Devon.
Stuart Boam	Manager of Kodak (films), then a newsagent.
Peter Brine	Gaming machines manager for a major casino.
Arthur Brown	An accomplished sculptor.
Seth Buckley	Salt miner in Port Clarence.
Don Burluraux	Worked in a shoe-box-making factory.
Neville Chapman	Tanker driver; killed in a road accident in 1993, aged fifty-two.
Jimmy Cochrane	Became a solicitor for a Darlington law firm.
Alan Comfort	Entered clergy, became Church of England vicar in Co. Durham.
Eddie Connachan	Plumber in South Africa.
Bob Corbett	Deeply involved in pigeon racing (a fancier).
Stephen Corden	Structural engineer in Yarm with university degree.
James Cowan	Now a policeman on Teeside.
Pat Cuff	Became a bookmaker, along with his brother.
Ian Davidson	Engaged as a salesman by Coca-Cola.
Stewart Davidson	Is a legal clerk by profession.
Billy Day	Bookmaker on Teeside.
Brian Deane	Sports Consultant, Blacks Solicitors LLP, Leeds.
Lindy Delaphena	Took job with a Jamaican broadcasting company.
Derrick Downing	Ran a nightclub and worked in a garage.
Chris Duffy	Qualified as a schoolteacher.
George Elliott	Cargo superintendent at Middlesbrough docks.
Willie Fernie	Ran his own taxi firm in Glasgow.
Jan-Age Fjortoft	Sporting Director of Lillestrøm FC, Norway.
Alan Foggon	Worked for Tyneside security firm.
Bill Gates	Invested in a sports business; later retired to the Caribbean.
Ian Gibson	Worked at Port Stanley airport, Falkland Islands; also on oil rigs.
Gary Gill	BBC Radio Cleveland reporter; buyer for men's leisurewear chain.
Tom Green	Wireless operator at Cable & Wireless, Aldershot.
Tom Griffiths	Director of Wrexham FC; also an accomplished cellist.

Craig Harrison	Opened a pet training centre in the North East.
Harry Harrison	Fishmonger in Redcar for many years.
John Hickton	Entered into the insurance business in Chesterfield.
Walter Holmes	Lay preacher who regularly conducted sportsmen's services.
Arthur Horsfield	Became a Gravesend postman and managed a social club.
Teddy Howling	Commission Agent's clerk in South Bank.
Bosco Jankovic	Ran his own law practice in Yugoslavia before war hit the country.
Jack Jennings	Trained the England Amateur XI; physio for Northants CC.
Craig Johnson	Journalist, football boot designer, songwriter.
Ian Johnson	Worked for Sunderland Housing Department and sold insurance.
Chris Kamara	Soccer pundit on Sky Sports.
Arthur Kaye	A joiner/carpenter.
Fred Kennedy	Ran tobacconist's shop in Manchester.
Paul Kerr	Financial Advisor, commentator for Radio Cleveland
Fred Kirby	Surveyor for Morpeth Rural District Council.
Owen McGhee	Gained a maths degree at University of Teeside.
John McLean	Took up bricklaying.
Eric McMordie	Went into business on Teeside.
Mick McNeil	Opened sports outfitter's in Suffolk.
George Martin	Accomplished sculptor.
Brian Marwood	Chairman of the PFA and radio broadcaster.
Paul Merson	Soccer pundit on Sky Sports.
Danny Mills	Soccer broadcaster/summariser.
David Mills	Engaged as a rep for printing company; also a coach and scout.
Chris Morris	Set up a Cornish pasty business.
Robbie Mustoe	College coaching & media work, Lexington, Massachusetts, USA.
Frank Nash	Chairman of the South Bank & Hemlington Social Club.
Irving Nattress	Has a retail clothing business in Chester-le-Street & Gateshead.

Olly Norris	Australian Soccer Federation coach, based in Victoria.
Mel Nurse	Joined Swansea City as Director; ran country club hotel in city.
Keith O'Neill	Entered into the Christmas cracker business.
Tony O'Rourke	Newsagent on South Coast.
Robert Page	Bookbinder for Jordisons.
Gary Pallister	Sky Sports Soccer pundit.
Gary Parkinson	Gained coaching certificate with the FA.
Alan Peacock	Newsagent and businessman, ex-Boro Players' Association.
Andy Peake	Police officer in Leicestershire force.
Stephen Pears	Housebuilder and goalkeeping coach.
Fred Pentland	Respected football coach in France and Spain.
Tom Phillipson	Teacher in Spennymoor.
Jamie Pollock	Entered into the glassmaking business.
Mark Proctor	Qualified as an FA coach.
Stan Rickaby	Accountant, insurance broker, ice cream salesman.
Dicky Rooks	Builder in Sunderland.
Dicky Robinson	Furness shipyard worker.
Maurice Short	Ventured into being a grocer.
Bernie Slaven	Radio and TV soccer pundit.
Alex Smith	Middlesbrough's kit man since 1996.
Malcolm Smith	Hi-Tec sales representative.
Jim Sphuler	Ran Yarm post office for eight years.
Jim Stewart	Ministry of Defence policeman in Kilmarnock.
Andy Townsend	ITV football match summariser
Rolando Ugolini	Bookmaker in Edinburgh.
Tommy Urwin	Accounts clerk in Sunderland Royal Infirmary.
Stan Vickers	Entered into property development.
Russell Wainscoat	Railway clerk, shoe shop owner, confectioner, publican.
Bob Walker	Sports-master at a public school in Essex.
John Walker	Ran fish shop in Swindon.
Maurice Webster	Dorman Long's Port Clarence works.
Bill Whittaker	Coal-miner, having earlier been a Bevin Boy.
Alf Wood	Ran his own business, West Midlands Promotions.
Christian Ziege	Director of Football at Borussia Mönchengladbach (2007).

Alan Comfort was also a vicar in East London and later served as Chaplain at Leyton Orient FC. Jack Jennings also coached/trained the GB team at three Olympic Games and worked at three local schools;. Ian Gibson was also engaged as a scaffold worker in Holland and ran a hairdressing salon in Redcar, and several ex-Middlesbrough players worked at ICI Wilton. Brian Deane also managed a Norwegian football club.

NAME GAME

Among the players with the longest names (overall) who have appeared in competitive matches for Middlesbrough we have: William Murdoch Morrison Whigham (29 letters), Frederick Beaconsfield Pentland (28), George Francis Moutry Hardwick (27), Michael Francis Martin Kennedy (27), Claudio Ibraim Vaz Leal Branco (26), Seamus Cyril Patrick O'Connell (26), Abel Luis Silva Costa Xavier (26), George Arthur Heads Emmerson (25), Ahmed Hossam Abdel Hamid Mido (25), Dimitrios Konstantopoulos (24), Thomas William Steel Watkin (24), Reginald Garnet Williamson (24).

Those with the shortest names include: John Kay (7 letters), Hugh Caig (8), Uwe Fuchs (8), Gary Gill (8), John Hogg (8), John Muir (8), John Wark (8), Julio Arca (9), James Bell (9), Henry Kent (9), Brian Laws (9), Alan Moody (9), Colin Ross (9), Alan Walsh (9), Gary Walsh (9), James Weir (9) and Alan White (9).

LONG AND THE SHORT

Of the many tall players who have appeared in first-class matches for Middlesbrough we have (from A–Z): Harry Allport, Joe Blackett, 1960s full-back Peter Bryan (6 foot 5 inches), Christian Burgess (6 foot 5 inches), Ben Davies (goalkeeper, 1912), Joe Gettins, Herold Goulon (6 foot 4 inches), goalkeepers Jim Mathieson (1927) and Esmond Million, Joe Murphy, Ron Patterson (6 foot 5 inches), Eddie Russell (1953), Ross Turnbull (6 foot 4 inches), Mark Schwarzer

(6 foot 4 inches), David Wheater (6 foot 5 inches) and Bill Whitaker (1949).

Those of the shorter brigade include: probably the smallest of them all, Stephen Spriggs, at 5 foot 3 inches, followed by 1936s star Ray Bryan (5 foot 4 inches), 1950s winger Arthur Kaye (5 foot 6 inches), 1949/50 inside-forward Peter Desmond (5 foot 6 inches), 1926–31 right-half Joe Miller (5 foot 6 inches), early 1900s right-winger Martin Moran (5 foot 6 inches), utility forward Tommy Urwin (5 foot 5 inches) and Fred Warren from 1933/34 (5 foot 5 inches).

HOLDING THE 'BORO FORT

Over the years, there have been some quite outstanding goalkeepers to occupy the last line of defence for Middlesbrough football club, with Reginald Garnet 'Tim' Williamson by far the greatest of them all. He amassed 603 first team appearances for the club between 1901 and 1923. Others include Bob Appleby (110), Jack Clough (128), Ted Connachan (105), Dave Cumming (157), Jim Mathieson (264), Stephen Pears (424), Jim Platt (481), Mark Schwarzer (445), Jason Steele (130), Peter Taylor (146) and Rolando Ugolini (335).

Schwarzer, who reached the career milestone of 750 club appearances in 2014, has also played in 109 full internationals for Australia.

Bob Anderson conceded seven goals on his League debut for 'Boro against Arsenal in front of 57,557 spectators at Highbury in March 1948. He was said to have been at fault for five of them and as a result never played for the first team again.

Walter Briggs conceded four on his League debut for 'Boro against Grimsby Town at Blundell Park in May 1947.

Middlesbrough 'keeper Ben Roberts is on record for having conceded the fastest-ever FA Final Cup, beaten by Roberto Di Matteo's looping drive after just 42 seconds of the Wembley encounter with Chelsea in May 1997.

Kevin Poole, who made 42 appearances for Middlesbrough between 1987 and 1990, was born in July 1963 and was still a registered professional with Burton Albion in 2014, aged forty-one.

ON HIGH GROUND

Middlesbrough have played a total of 45 games on the highest ground in the Football League, The Hawthorns, home of West Bromwich Albion, which stands 551 feet above sea level. Oldham Athletic's Boundary Park comes next at 526 feet, with Vale Park (home of Port Vale) at 520 feet.

'Boro first travelled to The Hawthorns on Saturday 14 December 1901, for a mid-season Second Division fixture, which they lost 2-0 in front of 6,868 spectators.

'Boro's first win at the Black Country ground followed on 5 February 1921 when they beat the reigning League champions 1-0 with a George Elliott goal.

In fact, Elliott was the first 'Boro player to score at 'altitude' in a 3-1 League defeat at The Hawthorns in April 1912 (Division One). Future 'Boro star Steve Bloomer had the distinction of scoring the first-ever League goal at The Hawthorns for Derby County against West Brom in September 1900. This is 'Boro's full record versus the Baggies:

	P	W	D	L	F	A
FL/PL	43	10	9	24	41	70
FA Cup	2	0	1*	1	1	2
Total	45	10	10	25	42	72

*This drawn match was in the fifth round of the FA Cup in February 2005, which 'Boro went on to win 5-4 on penalties at The Hawthorns.

GEORGE HARDWICK: TOP MAN

George Hardwick (2 February 1920–19 April 2004) was an exceptionally fine left-back who later became a successful coach. During his time as a player with Middlesbrough (May 1937–November 1950), he made 166 League and FA Cup appearances, played in 39 Second World War games and won thirteen full caps for England, serving both club and country as captain. In 1947, the Nations of Great Britain joined together to form a football team, which Hardwick captained and led to victory (6-1) against the Rest of Europe XI. After his Middlesbrough career was over, Hardwick became player-manager of Oldham Athletic and thereafter took charge of PSV Eindhoven and, from 1959 to 1961, bossed the Netherlands national football team. He later managed Sunderland and Gateshead.

Today, Hardwick's legacy lives on in the form of The George Hardwick Foundation, a charity dedicated to helping carers, former carers and patients. The patron is his wife, Jennifer, who cared for George during his latter years. They have three main sites at Stockton, Middlesbrough and The University Hospital of North Tees.

GREAT TRAIN ROBBER

In 1963, Middlesbrough's Welsh international defender Mel Nurse was detained by police, who suspected him of being one of the Great Train robbers. He was released without charge.

MISSING TELEGRAM!

In 1920, Middlesbrough's Haswell-born inside-forward Tommy Urwin was sent a telegram by the FA informing he had been chosen to play for England. Unfortunately, he never received the telegram and when he never answered, the FA selected Derby County's Alf Quantrill instead.

LIFESAVER

Fred Kennedy, an inside-right with Middlesbrough during seasons 1927–29, saved the life of a drowning woman and was awarded a certificate by the Royal Humane Society for his brave effort.

NAP HANDS

Four players, one of whom achieved the feat twice, share the record for scoring most goals in a Football League game for Middlesbrough. All netted five times and they are:

John Wilkie	*v.* Gainsborough Trinity, Division Two (2 March 1901)
Andy Wilson	*v.* Nottingham Forest, Division One (6 October 1923)
George Camsell	*v.* Manchester City, Division Two (25 December 1926)
George Camsell	*v.* Aston Villa, Division One (9 September 1935)
Brian Clough	*v.* Brighton & Hove Albion, Division Two (22 August 1956)

Jimmy McClelland netted all of Middlesbrough's goals in their 5-1 FA Cup home win over Leeds United in January 1926.

DOUBLE CELEBRATION

On 4 October 2008, Jérémie Aliadière's 89th minute winner for Middlesbrough against Wigan Athletic sealed the club's first away win of that year and the goal itself was 'Boro's 600th in the Premiership.

TOP GOLFERS

Tom Woodward, a 'Boro player for two seasons, from 1949 to 1951, won the PGA golf championship in Liverpool in October 1950. Besides being a fine full-back with 'Boro, making over 400 appearances between 1945 and 1959, Dicky Robinson was also a very good golfer, completing in the PFA Championships in 1951 when his manager at Ayresome Park, David Jack, carried his clubs.

BOWLED OVER

Ex-Middlesbrough goalscorer Andy Wilson represented England at bowls in 1948. He also played billiards and snooker and was no mean golfer either.

LONG SERVICE

Goalkeeper 'TiM' Williamson served Middlesbrough for a total of twenty-two years (1901–23). He was thirty-eight years and nine months old when he played his last game for the club against Cardiff City on 24 March 1923. He was the oldest player to appear for 'Boro at that time and it would be another seventy-four years before his record was broken by Bryan Robson in 1997.

MAKING CONTACT

Left-winger Bob Hume was one of the first footballers to wear contact lenses in a competitive game. He wore spectacles at school (in Scotland) and soon after joining Glasgow Rangers in 1959, he began to use lenses. He joined Middlesbrough in 1962 and later played for Aberdeen before moving to South Africa. Sadly, Hume was murdered in 1997, the victim of a carjacking as he drove to his Johannesburg home. He was just fifty-six.

MEDAL WINNERS

Bobby Murdoch won nineteen medals at club level; midfielders Bryan Robson and Brazilian Juninho both gained twelve, while Gordon Strachan and Paul Ince collected eleven apiece.

KITTED OUT

Since the 2009/10 season, Middlesbrough's kit has been produced by Adidas, replacing the previous deal with Errea which had lasted for fifteen years. The kit is only available in the UK from the official club shops and Middlesbrough's online store. The club's shirt sponsor was announced in July 2007 as satellite navigation device manufacturers Garmin. The initial contract was then extended until the end of the 2008/09 season in a deal described as 'the biggest in the club's history'. As of the start of the 2011/12 season, Middlesbrough FC has been sponsored by Ramsdens pawnbrokers.

Official Kit Manufacturers

1976/77	Bukta
1977–83	Adidas
1984–87	Hummel
1987–92	Skill
1992–94	Admiral
1994–2009	Errea
2009–present	Adidas

Kit Sponsors (For Club Shirts)

1980–82	Datsun Cleveland
1982–84	McLean Homes
1984–86	Camerons
1986–88	Dickens
1988–90	Heritage Hampers
1990–92	*Evening Gazette*
1992–94	ICI
1994–95	Dickens
1995–2002	Cellnet/BT Cellnet
2002–04	Dial a Phone
2004–07	888.com
2007–10	Garmin
2011–present	Ramsdens

NOT ENGLISH!

As at 2014, more than 130 non-English players from thirty-seven different countries appeared for Middlesbrough at senior level. So far there have been twenty-five Scots, twenty-one players from the Republic of Ireland, nine Australians, eight Brazilians, six Dutch, six French, five from Italy, Northern Ireland and Wales, four Argentineans, four Germans, four Nigerians, three Cameroonians, three Spaniards, two Egyptians, two Jamaicans and two Slovakians, plus one from Austria, Belgium, Bolivia, Colombia, Croatia, Denmark, Estonia, Ghana, Greece, Hungary, Morocco, New Zealand, Norway, Portugal, Senegal, Sierra Leone, South Korea, Switzerland, Trinidad & Tobago and Turkey.

CRICKETING FOOTBALLERS

Several footballers who appeared for Middlesbrough were also pretty good with the little red ball, and included among them we have Harry Bell (Durham and Middlesbrough CC in North Yorkshire and South Durham Leagues), Ian Bell (Marske CC), Peter Creamer (England schoolboy cricketer), George Dews (Worcestershire CCC captain), Bob Ferguson (Bradford League), Vic Fox (Worcestershire, 1923–32), Don Gallagher (Middlesex CC, 1940s), Joe Gettins (Middlesex CCC), Alan Ramage (local clubs), Ben Roberts (Crook CC) and Jimmy Windridge (Warwickshire CCC wicketkeeper). Bell was also offered a contract by Somerset CCC.

Middlesbrough manager Wilf Gillow fielded as a substitute for England in a Test match against Australia at Old Trafford when a member of the Lancashire groundstaff.

HEAD TO HEAD

This is Middlesbrough's playing record against other clubs, in all competitions, excluding wartime fixtures and the three FL games played at the start of the 1939/40 season.

Opponents	P	W	D	L	F	A
Aberdeen	2	2	0	0	7	2
Accrington Stanley	1	0	0	1	1	2
AFC Bournemouth	13	6	1	6	24	13
Egaleo	1	1	0	0	1	0
Aldershot	1	1	0	0	2	1
Arsenal	129	33	33	63	154	207
AS Roma	2	1	1	0	2	1
Aston Villa	139	42	33	64	176	244
AZ Alkmaar	1	0	1	0	0	0
Banik Ostrava	2	1	1	0	4	1
Barnet	2	2	0	0	3	0
Barnsley	56	29	11	16	102	54
Barrow	1	1	0	0	2	1
Birmingham City	107	31	32	44	134	161
Bishop Auckland	4	4	0	0	11	2
Bishop's Stortford	2	1	1	0	4	3
Blackburn Rovers	127	38	32	57	164	207
Blackpool	64	28	16	20	112	95
Bolton Wanderers	121	39	31	51	174	189
Bradford City	46	21	10	15	64	59
Bradford Park Ave	12	3	2	7	20	24
Brentford	17	7	3	7	25	20
Brighton & Hove Albion	42	22	11	9	78	43
Bristol City	73	30	22	21	98	82
Bristol Rovers	26	12	5	9	46	43
Burnley	62	22	17	23	97	104
Burton Albion	1	0	0	1	1	2
Burton Swifts	6	3	1	2	24	9
Bury	48	19	13	16	81	67
Cambridge United	4	0	2	2	1	4
Cardiff City	57	18	11	28	73	85
Carlisle United	32	14	5	13	37	35
Charlton Athletic	100	41	24	35	148	137
Chelsea	114	31	29	54	126	173
Chester City	2	1	0	1	3	3
Chesterfield	21	11	4	6	41	29
Colchester United	3	3	0	0	11	4
Coventry City	47	16	15	16	63	58

Crewe Alexandra	2	1	1	0	2	1
Crystal Palace	47	17	12	18	60	63
Darlington	10	7	2	1	23	7
Derby County	138	60	30	48	247	200
Dnepr	1	1	0	0	3	0
Doncaster Rovers	24	16	3	5	56	20
Ecclesfield	2	1	0	1	3	2
Everton	119	33	35	61	164	216
FC Basel	2	1	0	1	4	3
Fulham	58	27	9	22	92	76
Gainsborough Trinity	7	4	2	1	19	11
Gateshead N. E. R.	1	1	0	0	2	1
Gillingham	5	2	2	1	7	6
Glossop	4	1	1	2	10	5
Goole Town	1	1	0	0	9	3
Grantham Town	1	1	0	0	2	0
Grasshoppers	1	1	0	0	1	0
Graz	2	1	1	0	4	3
Grimsby Town	61	27	19	32	136	116
Halifax Town	3	3	0	0	7	1
Hallam	1	1	0	0	6	0
Hartlepool United	2	1	1	0	3	1
Hebburn Athletic	3	1	0	2	3	9
Hednesford Town	1	1	0	0	3	2
Hereford United	3	3	0	0	14	0
Howden Rangers	1	1	0	0	4	1
Huddersfield Town	88	37	19	32	136	116
Hull City	58	25	17	16	93	75
Ipswich Town	62	18	14	30	77	99
Jarrow	3	2	0	1	7	2
Kettering Town	1	1	0	0	5	0
Lanerossi Vicenza	2	1	1	0	4	2
Leadgate Exiles	1	1	0	0	4	2
Leeds United	91	30	26	35	129	141
Leicester City	90	29	26	35	128	126
Leyton Orient	40	16	9	15	62	60
Lincoln City	23	10	7	6	42	38
Litets FC	1	1	0	0	2	0
Liverpool	141	41	39	61	179	240

Loughborough Town	2	1	1	0	4	1
Luton Town	27	9	6	12	30	42
Macclesfield Town	2	2	0	0	5	2
Manchester City	125	48	27	50	185	175
Manchester United	123	33	28	62	166	214
Mansfield Town	11	6	2	3	19	14
Millwall	40	20	11	18	66	60
New Brighton	4	2	1	1	9	7
Newark	1	1	0	0	4	1
Newcastle United	127	40	38	49	156	185
Newport County	2	2	0	0	3	0
Northampton Town	7	5	1	1	14	7
Norwich City	48	19	13	16	74	57
Nottingham Forest	77	21	32	24	108	110
Notts County	66	31	10	25	109	86
Nuneaton Borough	2	1	1	0	6	3
Old Etonians	1	0	0	1	2	5
Old Foresters	2	2	0	0	6	1
Oldham Athletic	59	20	9	21	64	72
Oxford United	26	15	6	5	44	27
Partizan Belgrade	1	1	0	0	3	0
Peterborough United	18	8	8	2	22	12
Plymouth Argyle	35	15	11	9	61	43
Portsmouth	111	42	31	38	175	160
Port Vale	33	17	6	10	63	42
Preston North End	91	41	21	29	143	116
Queens Park Rangers	45	13	15	17	58	76
Reading	25	9	9	7	34	25
Redcar	1	0	0	1	1	2
Rendel	2	2	0	0	5	0
Rochdale	1	0	1	0	0	0
Rotherham United	32	16	7	9	63	45
St Augustine's	1	1	0	0	4	1
SC Lazio	1	1	0	0	2	0
Scarborough	3	3	0	0	19	2
Scunthorpe United	18	10	4	4	37	19
Sevilla	1	0	0	1	0	4
Sheffield United	101	38	22	41	147	140
Sheffield Wednesday	102	41	17	44	172	156

Shrewsbury Town	15	9	3	3	29	12
South Bank	3	2	0	1	10	7
South Shields	6	2	3	1	10	5
Southampton	55	17	15	23	78	88
Southend United	6	3	1	2	6	4
Southport	1	1	0	0	3	0
Sporting Lisbon	2	0	0	2	2	4
Staveley Town	1	0	0	1	1	5
Steaua Bucharest	2	1	0	1	4	3
Stockport County	13	9	3	1	28	7
Stoke City	92	38	20	34	137	122
Sunderland	143	46	37	60	184	207
Sutton United	2	1	1	0	2	1
Swansea City	42	18	9	15	90	69
Swindon Town	30	16	5	9	48	30
Torquay United	2	1	0	1	5	2
Tottenham Hotspur	91	34	24	33	147	141
Tow Law	1	1	0	0	3	0
VfB Stuttgart	2	1	0	1	2	2
Villarreal	1	0	0	1	0	2
Walsall	15	6	4	5	24	16
Watford	34	14	6	14	46	41
West Brom Albion	91	37	21	33	118	111
West Ham United	64	24	14	26	87	81
Whitburn	1	1	0	0	4	0
Wigan Athletic	13	5	6	2	13	9
Willington Athletic	5	3	2	0	17	5
Wimbledon	27	7	12	8	23	26
Wolverhampton W.	87	41	20	26	140	128
Workington	2	2	0	0	5	3
Wrexham	1	0	0	1	1	2
Wycombe Wanderers	2	1	1	0	1	0
Xanthi	2	1	1	0	2	0
Yeovil Town	3	3	0	0	13	3
York City	11	3	4	4	17	14

Where games went to a penalty shoot-out, the score in open play has been recorded. Clubs who have changed their name over the course of time, or indeed, added a name to their initial title, are given as they are at

2014 (including Clapton/Leyton Orient, Chester/City, Leicester Fosse/City, Newton Heath/Manchester United, Small Heath/Birmingham City, Stoke/City, Swansea Town/City, Woolwich Arsenal/Arsenal).

PADDY WEDS A SWIMMER

Chris 'Paddy' Johnson, who played for 'Boro in the late 1940s, making just two appearances, married the famous British Channel swimmer Brenda Fisher, who set a record time of 12 hours and 42 minutes to cover the 21-mile stretch from Dover to Calais in 1951. This was 73 minutes faster than the previous record and she was awarded £1,000 by the *Daily Mail* for her bold effort.

COMMUNITY SCHEME

Middlesbrough FC in the Community (MFCIC) was founded in 1995 by club chairman Steve Gibson and in 2014 was regarded as the largest community-based football scheme in the United Kingdom. Run separately from the football club, it receives support from the club in terms of providing players, staff, stadium facilities and PR in the matchday programme and other publications, as well as support from other local organisations. Since 2002, the club and MFCIC have also run the Middlesbrough Enterprise Academy, a scheme that helps local children improve their entrepreneurial skills and increase their awareness of business planning and finance. In March 2008, plans were announced by the Premier League to roll out the scheme nationally among all Premier League clubs. Three months before that, in December 2007, Middlesbrough stated that the club had carried out more community work during the 2006/07 season than any other Premier League club, rising from second place the previous year, with the club making 318 appearances – almost twice the Premier League average of 162. They were in the top two for community appearances again in 2007/08, with 374, a 17 per cent increase on the previous season.

UPS AND DOWNS

Middlesbrough have so far been promoted on ten occasions and also been relegated ten times. This is their yo-yo record:

1902	Promoted to FL1	1986	Relegated to FL3
1924	Relegated to FL2	1987	Promoted to FL2
1927	Promoted to FL1	1988	Promoted to FL1
1928	Relegated to FL2	1989	Relegated to FL2
1929	Promoted to FL1	1992	Promoted to PL
1954	Relegated to FL2	1993	Relegated to FL1
1966	Relegated to FL3	1995	Promoted to PL
1967	Promoted to FL2	1997	Relegated to FL1
1974	Promoted to FL1	1998	Promoted to the PL
1982	Relegated to FL2	2009	Relegated to the FLC

Boro's first promotion campaign in 1901/02 saw then finish runners-up behind West Bromwich Albion, who won both League games between the clubs, 2-1 at Linthorpe Road and 2-0 at The Hawthorns. The star of 'Boro's defence was Abe Jones, who had been signed from the Baggies in May 1901.

I'M IN CHARGE!

Since joining the Football League in 1899, Middlesbrough have had thirty-five different managers, including four on a caretaker (interim) basis, while two of them – Bryan Robson and Terry Venables – shared the role for the second half (six months) of the 2000/01 season. The thirty-five 'Boro bosses are listed here:

Term of Office	Name	P	W	D	L
May 1899–May 1905	John Robson	215	82	47	86
June 1905–October 1906	Alex Mackie	52	13	15	24
November 1906–Feb 1909	Andy Aitken	95	40	18	37
February 1909–June 1910	John Gunter	79	28	19	35
June 1910–January 1911	Andy Walker	20	9	7	4
August 1911–December 1919	Tom McIntosh	179	69	42	68

April 1920–July 1923	Jimmy Howie	132	47	37	48
August 1923–January 1927	Herbert Bamlett	110	30	27	53
January 1927–March 1934	Peter McWilliam	328	132	75	121
March 1934–March 1944	Wilf Gillow	236	92	55	89
November 1944–April 1952	David Jack	270	100	61	109
June 1952–February 1954	Walter Rowley	73	22	16	35
July 1954–January 1963	Bob Dennison	381	158	77	146
January 1963–February 1966	Raich Carter	143	46	41	56
April 1966–January 1973	Stan Anderson	332	139	89	104
January 1973–May 1973	Harold Shepherdson*	17	9	4	4
May 1973–April 1977	Jack Charlton	193	88	49	56
May 1977–July 1981	John Neal	196	69	52	75
June 1981–October 1982	Bobby Murdoch	54	9	19	26
October 1982–March 1984	Malcolm Allison	77	24	24	29
March 1984–June 1984	Jack Charlton	9	3	3	3
June 1984–February 1986	Willie Maddren	77	17	20	44
February 1986–March 1990	Bruce Rioch	205	82	52	71
March 1990–June 1991	Colin Todd	70	28	16	26
July 1991–May 1994	Lennie Lawrence	157	61	43	53
May 1994–December 2000	Bryan Robson	314	127	86	101
December 2000–May 2001	Robson/ Terry Venables	25	8	11	6
June 2001–May 2006	Steve McClaren	250	97	60	93
June 2006–October 2009	Gareth Southgate	151	45	43	63
October 2009 for three days	Colin Cooper*	1	0	1	0
October 2009–October 2010	Gordon Strachan	51	15	13	23
October 2010 for seven days	Steve Agnew*	2	0	0	2
October 2010–October 2013	Tony Mowbray	153	61	37	55
October 2013–Nov 2013	Mark Venus*	3	1	1	1
November 2013–present	Aitor Karanka	32	13	9	10

*Shepherdson, Cooper, Agnew and Venus were all in charge on a caretaker basis.

BOSS'S NOTEPAD

1. John Robson kept goal for 'Boro's second XI.

2. Mackie, who never played professional football, also managed Sunderland.

3. Aitken was a former Newcastle United 'great' who made 345 appearances for the Magpies and played for Scotland.

4. Walker was suspended for making an illegal approach to an Airdrieonians player and was subsequently out of football for eighteen years, from 1911 to 1929.

5. McIntosh played for and managed Darlington; served in France during the First World War and returned to become secretary-manager of Everton, signing Dixie Dean.

6. Howie, known as 'Gentleman Jim', scored 83 goals in 235 games for Newcastle and won three caps for Scotland. He also managed QPR (before 'Boro).

7. Bamlett refereed the 1914 FA Cup final between Burnley and Liverpool. He also managed Oldham Athletic, Wigan Borough and Manchester United.

8. McWilliam excelled as a player and also as a manager. He starred for Newcastle United, winning an FA Cup and three League championship medals, and for Scotland before taking over as manager of Tottenham Hotspur. He also served as a scout for Arsenal.

9. Gillow played for Blackpool, Grimsby Town and Preston and also bossed Grimsby, and once fielded as a substitute for England against Australia in an Ashes Test at Old Trafford.

10. Jack scored the first-ever Wembley goal for Bolton Wanderers against West Ham United in the 1923 FA Cup final. He was also involved in a British transfer record when he was signed

by Arsenal from Bolton for £10,890 in 1928. Capped nine times by England, Jack also managed the Irish club Shelbourne and after retiring worked for the Air Ministry.

11. Rowley gave Bolton Wanderers thirty-eight years' service as a player, coach and manager before bossing Middlesbrough. He also managed Shrewsbury Town (1955–57).

12. Dennison played for Newcastle Uunited, Nottingham Forest, Fulham and Northampton Town before taking his first managerial post with the latter. He sued Middlesbrough for unfair dismissal. He won his case and was awarded £3,200 in damages. Dennison later acted as chief scout and caretaker and also assistant manager at Coventry City.

13. Carter was one of the great inside-forwards of the later 1930s. An England international, he starred for Sunderland before the hostilities and after the Second World War appeared for Derby County and Hull City, whom he also managed. He was also placed in charge of Leeds United and Mansfield Town.

14. Anderson was an England international wing-half who played for Newcastle United and Sunderland, making over 400 appearances for the latter. He was player-coach at 'Boro before taking over as manager. He was later employed in various capacities, by AEK Athens, QPR, Manchester City, Doncaster Rovers and Bolton Wanderers.

15. Charlton, OBE, a World Cup winner in 1966 and the recipient of 35 England caps, made 629 appearances for Leeds United between 1953 and 1973. He was Footballer of the Year in 1967 but was often overshadowed by his brother, Bobby. Charlton also managed the Republic of Ireland and Newcastle United (1984).

16. Neal was a full-back with Hull City, King's Lynn, Swindon Town, Aston Villa and Southend before entering management with Wrexham (1968). He managed Chelsea after leaving 'Boro.

17. Murdoch won eight League titles, eight Scottish Cup finals, eight League Cup finals and the 1967 European Cup with Celtic. A brilliant wing-half, he made 291 League appearances north of the border before moving to Middlesbrough, initially as a player in 1973.

18. Allison was a player with Charlton Athletic and West Ham before managing Bath City and then Plymouth Argyle, followed by further appointments at Manchester City (in Partnership with Joe Mercer), Crystal Palace and Galatasaray. After his spell in charge of 'Boro he went off to Kuwait and then Portugal and later had a stint as manager of Bristol Rovers (1992/93).

19. Maddren made 354 senior appearances for 'Boro before taking over as manager at Ayresome Park when the club was 1.2 million in debt. Sadly, Maddren was struck down with motor neurone disease and died at the age of forty-nine in 2000.

20. Rioch was an attacking wing-half who starred for Luton Town, Aston Villa, Derby County, Everton, Birmingham City, Sheffield United, Seattle Sounders (NASL) and Scotland, gaining twenty-four full caps and making more than 600 club appearances in total. He also managed Millwall, Arsenal, Bolton Wanderers, Norwich City, Wigan Athletic and Torquay United.

21. Todd was a class defender who played for Sunderland, Derby County, Nottingham Forest, Birmingham City, Oxford United, Vancouver Whitecaps and Luton Town, as well as England, gaining twenty-seven full caps. He also managed Whitley Bay, Bolton Wanderers, Swindon Town and his former club, Derby County. He amassed over 800 appearances during his twenty-one-year playing career.

22. Lawrence had managed Charlton Athletic for eight years before taking over at 'Boro. Later boss of Bradford City, Luton Town, Grimsby Town and Cardiff City, he also served as Director of Football with Bristol Rovers.

23. Robson, OBE, was one of the game's greatest competitors. He made 249 appearances for West Bromwich Albion (46 goals) and 465 for Manchester United (100 goals) before joining Middlesbrough as player-manager in 1994. After leaving 'Boro, 'Pop' returned to Old Trafford as a coach and later bossed his former club, WBA (saving the Baggies from relegation from the Premiership), as well as Sheffield United, Bradford City and the Thailand national team. He won 90 full caps for England, representing his country in three World Cups, scoring one of the quickest-ever goals in the 1982 tournament in Spain, netting after just 27 seconds against France. His brother, Gary, also played for WBA.

24. Venables had played for Chelsea, Tottenham Hotspur, Queens Park Rangers, Crystal Palace and St Patrick's Athletic between 1960 and 1977, making 512 League appearances, as well as winning two full England caps. 'El Tel' had managed Palace, QPR, Barcelona (1984–87), Spurs, England (1994–96), Australia and Palace (again) before assisting Bryan Robson at Middlesbrough. In 2012, he was appointed Technical Advisor at Wembley.

25. McClaren, a Yorkshireman, played for Hull City, Derby County, Lincoln City, Bristol City and Oxford United before becoming a coach with the latter club. He then served as assistant-manager at Derby and Manchester United (under Sir Alex Ferguson) before moving into management with Middlesbrough and thereafter with England (2006–08). Since then he has taken charge of FC Twente (twice), VfL Wolfsburg, Nottingham Forest and Derby County, the latter since 2013.

26. Southgate joined Middlesbrough as a player from Aston Villa for £6.5 million in 2001, and in 2004 became the first captain of the club to lift a major trophy (the Football League Cup). His reign as 'Boro manager wasn't great and since his departure he has worked as a soccer pundit on television and also for the FA. He won fifty-seven caps for England but suffered the disappointment and criticism after missing a vital spot-kick in the penalty shoot-out against Germany at Euro '96.

27. Cooper was in charge of 'Boro for just one match – a 2-2 draw *v.* Preston North End in October 2009. A defender of the highest class, he made over 600 League appearances while playing for Middlesbrough (two spells), Millwall, Nottingham Forest and Sunderland. He also won two England caps and has managed Bradford City and Hartlepool United.

28. Strachan, OBE, who won fifty full caps for Scotland and made well over 700 club appearances (635 at League level) while serving with Dundee, Aberdeen, Manchester United, Leeds United and Coventry City (1971–1997), went on to manage the Sky Blues, Southampton, Celtic, Middlesbrough and in 2014 was in charge of his country's national team.

29. Agnew made over 500 club appearances (436 in the League) between 1983 and 2002 with Barnsley, Blackburn Rovers, Portsmouth, Leicester City, Sunderland, York City and Gateshead before joining Middlesbrough as a coach, taking over briefly as caretaker-manager after Strachan's departure. At 2014 he was assistant-manager to Steve Bruce at Hull City.

30. Mowbray made 554 League appearances with three clubs: Middlesbrough (1982–91), Celtic (1991–95) and Ipswich Town (1995–2000). Since retiring he has managed Ipswich Town (interim), Hibernian, West Bromwich Albion, Celtic and 'Boro. A dedicated defender, he served 'Boro as a player and manager for thirteen years.

31. Venus was a left-back/centre-half with Hartlepool United, Leicester City, Wolves, Ipswich Town, Cambridge United, Dagenham & Redbridge and Hibernian: 1985–2004. In that time he accumulated 517 League appearances, 287 with Wolves. He was subsequently appointed as Mowbray's assistant at Hibs, West Brom, Celtic and 'Boro.

32. Karanka is the first foreigner to manage Middlesbrough. The Spaniard, born in 1973, was a defender with CF Corozonistas, CF Alaves, Athletic Bilbao (three spells) and Real Madrid

(1997–2002) in his homeland and Colorado Rapids (in the USA). He made over 400 club appearances (93 in La Liga with Real Madrid), and won fourteen U21 and four U23 caps for Spain, plus one at senior level. He also represented the Basque Country and had been assistant-manager of Real Madrid for three years before moving in as Middlesbrough manager.

PLAYER TO MANAGER

From the early years of the game scores of players, after retiring (some even before they took off their books) became a club manager, and Middlesbrough have certainly had plenty of footballers who wore the red-and-white strip make it into the world of management, some taking over at 'Boro. Here are a few, listed from A–Z:

Stan Anderson (Bolton Wanderers, Doncaster Rovers, Middlesbrough and in Greece), Viv Anderson (Barnsley), Billy Birrell (Chelsea, Raith Rovers), Joe Blackett (Rochdale), Clayton Blackmore (Porthmadog), Steve Bloomer (Britannia Berlin 92/Germany, Real Union/Spain), Stuart Boam (Mansfield Town), Joe Brown (Burnley), Jack Brownlie (Cowdenbeath), Geoff Butler (Salisbury City), Jacky Carr (Darlington, Tranmere Rovers), Brian Clough (Hartlepool United, Derby County, Brighton & Hove Albion, Leeds United, Nottingham Forest: 1975–93), Ernie 'Trim' Coleman (Notts County), Colin Cooper (Middlesbrough, caretaker-manage;r; Bradford City, caretaker-manager Hartlepool United), Terry Cooper (Birmingham City, Bristol City, Bristol Rovers, Exeter City, two spells), Bob Corbett (Brierley Hill), Peter Creamer (Whitby Town, Evenwood Town), Peter Davenport (Macclesfield Town, Southport, Colwyn Bay, Bangor City), Brian Deane (Sarpsborg 08/Norway), Stewart Davidson (Forres Mechanics/Scotland), Derrick Downing (Hatfield Main FC), David Hodgson (Darlington, two spells), Charlie Ferguson (Gateshead), Robert/Bob Ferguson (Northwich Victoria), Willie Fernie (Drogheda, Kilmarnock), Ray Freeman (Sheffield United, Rotherham United, Paul Gascoigne (Kettering Town), Ray Hankin (Darlington, Northallerton), George Hardwick (Gateshead, Sunderland), Bill Harris (Bradford City),

Charlie Hewitt (Millwall, two spells; Chester; Wrexham; Leyton Orient, Mold; Flint Town; Connah's Quay), Billy Horner (Darlington, Hartlepool United), Paul Ince (Blackpool, Blackburn Rovers, Macclesfield Town, MK Dons, two spells, Notts County), Chris Kamara (Bradford City), Harry Kent (Watford), Andy Kernaghan (Dundee), Cyril Knowles (Hartlepool United), Brian Laws (Grimsby Town, Scunthorpe United, Sheffield Wednesday), Jimmy Lawson (Halifax Town), George Martin (Aston Villa, Newcastle United), Don Masson (Kettering Town, LA Kickers), Alex McCrae (Stirling Albion, Ballymena), Paul Merson (Walsall), Jackie Mordue (Durham), Tony Mowbray (Hibernian, Middlesbrough, West Bromwich Albion), Bobby Murdoch (Middlesbrough), Charlie O'Hagan (Norwich City), Don O'Riordon (Torquay United), Nigel Pearson (Carlisle United; Newcastle United, two spells as caretaker-manager; Southampton; Hull City; Leicester City, two spells; West Bromwich Albion, caretaker-manager; England U21), Fred Pentland (Barrow, Brentford), Jim Platt (Darlington), Jamie Pollock (Spennymoor United), Mark Proctor (Livingston), Stan Rickaby (Weymouth), Bobby Robson ('Boro amateur; Vancouver Royals; Fulham; Ipswich Town; England 'B'; England national team; PSV Eindhoven, two spells; Sporting Lisbon, FC Porto; CF Barcelona; Newcastle United), Bryan Robson (Bradford City, Middlesbrough, Sheffield United, West Bromwich Albion, Thailand national team), Dicky Rooks (Scunthorpe United), Trevor Senior (Weymouth), Graeme Souness (Glasgow Rangers, Liverpool, Galatasaray, Southampton, Torino, Benfica, Blackburn Rovers, Newcastle United), Gareth Southgate (Middlesbrough, England U21), John Sphuler (Shrewsbury Town, Spennymoor United), Frank Spraggon (Reykjavik), Nobby Stiles (Preston North End, West Bromwich Albion, Vancouver Whitecaps), Jim Suddick (Nuneaton Borough), Peter Taylor (Burton Albion, Brighton & Hove Albion, Derby County), Paul Ward (Darlington), Andy Wilson (Clacton Town, Walsall).

Pentland was also successful as a coach/manager in Germany and Spain. Taylor was Brian Clough's assistant. Hodgson and Platt were joint managers at Darlington (1995). Hewitt was awarded £4,500 in damages in July 1956, after a great deal of publicity following his sacking as Millwall manager six months earlier.

BIG-MONEY TRANSFERS IN AND OUT AT 'BORO!

Top Signings

£12.8m	Afonso Alves	SC Heerenveen	January 2008
£8.15m	Massimo Maccarone	FC Empoli	July 2002
£8m	Ugo Ehiogu	Aston Villa	October 2000
£7.5m	Yakubu Ayegbeni	Portsmouth	July 2005
£7.1m	Fabrizio Ravanelli	Juventus	August 1996
£7m	Jonathan Woodgate	Real Madrid	April 2007
£6.5m	Gareth Southgate	Aston Villa	July 2001
£6m	Juninho Paulista	Atletico Madrid	July 2002
£6m	Robert Huth	Chelsea	August 2006
£6m	Mido	Tottenham Hotspur	August 2007
£5.25m	Nicky Barmby	Tottenham Hotspur	August 1995

Top Departures

£12m	Juninho Paulista	Atletico Madrid	July 1997
£12m	Stewart Downing	Aston Villa	July 2009
£11.25m	Yakubu Aiyegbeni	Everton	August 2007
£7m	Paul Merson	Aston Villa	September 1998
£7m	Afonso Alves	Al-Sadd	September 2009
£6m	Luke Young	Aston Villa	August 2008
£6m	Robert Huth	Stoke City	August 2009
£5.75m	Nick Barmby	Everton	October 1996
£5.5m	Christian Ziege	Liverpool	August 2000
£5.25m	Fabrizio Ravanelli	Olympique Marseille	August 1997
£5m	Sanli Tuncay	Stoke City	August 2009
£4.2m	Emerson Moises	CD Tenerife	January 1998
£4m	Lee Cattermole	Wigan Athletic	July 2008

MONEY TALK

Billy Ashcroft was Middlesbrough's first six-figure signing when bought for £135,000 from Wrexham in 1977. David Mills became the first half-a-million footballer in Britain when he left Middlesbrough for West Brom in January 1979 for a fee of £516,000 (signed by manager Ron Atkinson). Neil Cox was 'Boro's first £1 million player, signed from Aston Villa in 1994. When Villa recruited Cox from Scunthorpe United in 1991, they paid £400,000 – this was a record fee for a lower Division player. 'Boro defender Gary Pallister was sold to Manchester United for a club record £2.5m in 1989. In 2004, future Middlesbrough centre-back Jonathan Woodgate was sold by Newcastle United to Real Madrid for £13.2m. He joined 'Boro in 2006 (initially on loan).

NO GO ROLANDO

Celtic told Middlesbrough that they could not transfer their Italian-born goalkeeper Rolando Ugolini to another Scottish club. He eventually left Ayresome Park for Wrexham in 1956 and later he did move to Scotland, joining Dundee United in 1960.

GAZZA THE BEATLE

Paul Gascoigne was christened Paul John by his parents in tribute to two members of the famous Beatles – Paul McCartney and John Lennon. Why not Ringo or George, I wonder? Ringo Gascoigne would have been something to 'sing' about.

CLOUGH TAYLOR RIFT

Former Middlesbrough centre-forward Brian Clough and goalkeeper Peter Taylor were good friends (most of the time!). They played together for 'Boro from 1955 to 1960 and then worked in unison as manager and assistant-manager respectively at Hartlepool United, Derby County, Brighton and Hove Albion and Nottingham Forest. When Taylor retired from football in 1982, it brought to an end their long-standing partnership, which began in 1965.

Several events had started to strain their friendship when they worked at Derby together in the early 1970s. Indeed, Taylor was riled when he learned that Clough had accepted a pay rise from Rams' Chairman Sam Longson without telling him; Taylor did not get one. Then in 1980, Taylor released a book, entitled *With Clough, By Taylor*, which detailed their partnership, but he had not told Clough that he was writing it.

Surprisingly, six months after quitting the game, Taylor returned as Derby County's manager. And when the Rams met Clough's Forest in an FA Cup third-round tie in January 1983, the two managers ignored each other completely.

When Taylor signed left-winger John Robertson from Forest in June 1983 (without informing Clough), it was, according to Robertson, 'the straw that broke the camel's back'. The two men would never speak again.

In a tabloid article, Clough called Taylor a 'snake in the grass' and declared that 'if his car broke down and I saw him thumbing a lift, I wouldn't pick him up, I'd run him over'.

Taylor retorted that Clough's outbursts were 'the sort of thing I have come to expect from a person I now regard with great distaste'.

The rift had not been repaired by the time Taylor died in October 1990. However, Clough and his family did attend Taylor's funeral. According to Taylor's daughter, Wendy, Clough was 'deeply upset' by Taylor's death and telephoned her when he heard the news. Then, out of the blue, Clough chose to dedicate his autobiography, published in 1994, to Taylor. When he was given the Freedom of Nottingham, he also paid tribute to his former assistant, as he did in September 1999 when a bust was unveiled of himself at Nottingham Forest's City Ground.

CORRUPTION ALLEGATIONS

In the mid-1990s, Brian Clough was implicated in the famous 'bungs' scandal in English football. Under particular scrutiny was his involvement in the transfer of Teddy Sheringham from Nottingham Forest to Tottenham Hotspur in 1992. Spurs' chairman at that time,

Alan Sugar, claimed under oath to have been told by his then-manager Terry Venables that Clough 'liked a bung', an illicit payment made to ensure a transfer deal went through. Sugar sanctioned a cash payment of £58,750, which he believed would be paid to an agent, but instead it was handed over to Ronnie Fenton, Clough's assistant at Forest. Sugar, protected by legal immunity as a court witness, never repeated the allegation out of court during the rest of Clough's life. Clough was also alleged to have made illegal payments to players and backroom staff in breach of FA rules, something confirmed by former Forest chief scout Alan Hill. Clough denied the allegations, saying, 'Asking me what it's like to make money out of transfers is like asking "What's it like to have VD?" I don't know, I've never had it.'

Clough was charged with misconduct by the FA, who later dropped the case due to his poor health. Former Premier League Chief Executive, Rick Parry, who led the inquiry, said, 'On the balance of evidence, we felt he (Clough) was guilty of taking bungs. The evidence was pretty strong.'

CLOUGH THE MANAGER

As a manager, Brian Clough won sixteen trophies in twenty-two years between 1970 and 1992. He guided Derby County to the First Division title (1972), the Second Division championship (1969), Texaco Cup glory (also in 1972) and the Watney Cup (1970).

With Nottingham Forest, he also won the First Division title (1978), the League Cup on four occasions (1978, 1979, 1989 and 1990), the Simod Cup (1989), the Zenith Data Systems Cup (1992), the FA Charity Shield (1978), the European Cup (1979 and 1980), the European Super Cup (1979) and the Anglo-Scottish Cup (1977). He was also voted Manager of the Year in 1978.

You can also add to that impressive list, two runners-up prizes with Forest in the European Cup (1981) and FA Cup (1991) and League Cup semi-finalists with Derby (1968). He was boss of Hartlepool from 1965–67 (84 games in charge); Derby from 1967–73 (289 games at the helm); Brighton during season 1973–74 (32 matches), Leeds for 45 days, from July–September 1974 (7 fixtures) and Forest for eighteen years, from 1975 to May 1993 (907 games as manager). With five different clubs, Clough's managerial record was pretty good, giving him a win-rate of 45 per cent:

P	W	D	L
1,319	594	340	385

WEEKLY WAGE

When Middlesbrough joined the Football League in 1899, the maximum wage for a senior professional at the club was £4 a week. This payment remained as a fixed salary until 1910, when it rose by £1. Then, in 1920, a top-line footballer could earn up to £9 a week. However, a player's weekly salary was then reduced by £1 in 1922 and by 1930 it had dropped by another £1 to £7 a week. This remained the norm right up to 1945 when the maximum wage rose to £12 a week. Thereafter it went up steadily from £12, to £14, to £15, to £17, to £20 and then to £25 a week by 1961, when the maximum wage restriction was lifted. Although specific, cannot be revealed, some players in the 1960s and '70s were paid very well by the club, and it is common knowledge that certain international stars in the 1980s/'90s received as much as £500 a week, some as much as £1,000 a week. There is no doubt that players of today are very well paid, with bonuses thrown in for good measure, and if (or should that be when) Middlesbrough return to the Premiership, one feels that there will be a few millionaire footballers at the club.

FOREIGN BODIES

Over the course of time, certainly since 1899, Middlesbrough have recruited the services of over eighty foreign-born players, including:

Jeremie Aliadiere (France), Alfonso Alves (Brazil), Julio Arca (Argentina), Daniel Sánchez Ayala (Spain), Salif Bagayoko (Manosque, France), Mikkel Beck (Denmark), Arturo Benhardt (Santa Catarina, Brazil), Andre Bikey (Cameroon), George Boateng (Ghana/Holland), Alen Bokšić (Yugoslavia), Marco Branco (Italy), Claudio Ibraim Vaz Leal Branco (Brazil), Mustapha Carayol (Gambia), Benito Carbone (Italy), David Chadwick (India), Nathaniel Chalobah (Sierra Leone), Mikael Debeve (France), Lindy Delaphena (Jamaica), Didier Digard (France), Dorival Ghidoni/Doriva (Brazil), Marvin Emnet (Holland), Gianluca Festa (Sardinia/Italy), Jan-Age Fjortoft (Norway), Uwe Fuchs (Germany), Sorele Njitap Fotso Geremi (Cameroon), Harold Goulon (France), Maximilian Haas (Germany), Faris Haroun (Belgium), Jerrel/Jimmy Floyd Hasselbaink (Suriname), Robert Huth (Germany), Boško Janković (Yugoslavia), Chris Killen (New Zealand), Joseph-Désiré Job (France), Craig Johnston (South Africa), Bradley Jones (Australia), Oswaldo Giroldo Juninho (Brazil), Kei Kamara (Sierra Leone), Christian Karembeu (Lifou, New Caledonia), Vladimir Kinder (Slovakia), Chris Killen (New Zealand), Tarmo Kink (Estonia), Emmanuel Lesesma (Italy), Dong-Gook Lee (South Korea), Jayson Leutwiler (Switzerland), Arthur Lightening (South Africa), Leroy Lita (DR Congo), Gustavo Lombardi (Argentina), Scott McDonald (Australia), Massimo Maccarone (Italy), Mido (Egypt), Norman Malan (South Africa), Carlos Arturo Marinelli (Argentina), Dwight Marshall (Jamaica), Malaury Martin (France), Gaizka Mendieta (Spain), Emerson Costa Moises (Brazil), Fabio Da Silva Moreira (Brazil), Jaime Morales Moreno (Bolivia), Szilárd Németh (Slovakia), Niklas Nordgren (Sweden), Bart Ogbeche (Nigeria), Paul Okon (Australia), Kenneth Omerou (Nigeria), Hendrikus Matheus Otto (Holland), Bruno Pilatos (Angola), Manny Pogatetz (Austria), Franck Queudrue (France), Fabrizio Ravanelli (Italy), Michael John Reiziger (Holland), Hamilton Ricard Cuesta (Colombia), Ricardinho (Brazil), Fabio Rochemback (Brazil), Mark Schwarzer (Australia), Mohamed Shawky (Egypt), Mikael Tavares (Senegal), Sanli Tuncay (Turkey), Rolando Ugolini (Italy), Sergio Van Kanten (USA), Josef Varga (Hungary), Tony Vidmar (Australia), Mark Viduka (Australia), Luke Wilkshire (Australia), Rhys Williams (Perth, Australia), Abel Luis Da Silva Costa Xavier (Mozambique), Ayegbeni Yakubu (Nigeria), Merouane Zemmema (Morocco), Christian Ziege (Germany) and 'Bolo' Zenden (Holland).

RECORD LEAGUE WIN

On 23 August 1958, a crowd of 32,367 saw Middlesbrough record their biggest-ever League win, hammering Brighton & Hove Albion 9-0 at Ayresome Park in a Second Division match. Brian Clough (5), Bill Harris (2 penalties) and Alan Peacock (2) scored the goals.

PLAYER POWER

Middlesbrough had no less than fifty-two professionals on their books in 1999/2000, as well as sixteen trainees and one on a non-contract basis. Of these, seven (namely Branco, Festa, Kinder, Lombardi, Ricard, Schwarzer and Wiltshire) were born overseas while ten others were all originally from Dublin.

LONGEST GAMES

Middlesbrough have had several tightly contested, rather long, drawn-out FA Cup ties that have run to a third game, all but one of them involving a second replay. Here are details of 'Boro's eleven three-match fixtures:

1. Brighton & Hove Albion, FA Cup second round, February 1906
   (1-1, 1-1, won 3-1)

2. Charlton Athletic, FA Cup third round, January/February 1930
   (1-1, 1-1, won 1-0)

3. Bolton Wanderers, FA Cup third round, January 1939
   (0-0, 0-0, won 1-0)

4. Blackpool, FA Cup fourth round, January/February 1946
   (2-3, 3-2, won 2-1)

5. Aston Villa, FA Cup third round, January 1950
    (2-2, 0-0, won 3-0)

6. Hull City, League Cup second round, September/October 1962
    (2-2, 1-1, lost 0-3)

7. York City, FA Cup second round, January 1967
    (1-1, 0-0, won 4-1)

8. Hull City, FA Cup third round, January/February 1968
    (1-1, 2-2, won 1-0)

9. Tottenham Hotspur, League Cup 3rd round, October 1972
    (1-1, 0-0, lost 1-2)

10. Everton, FA Cup fourth round, January/February 1988
    (1-1, 2-2, lost 1-2)

11. Everton, FA Cup third round, January 1990
    (0-0, 1-1, lost 0-1)

The games against Charlton Athletic in FA Cup in 1930 and Tottenham Hotspur in the League Cup in 1972 are the two longest fixtures 'Boro have played, as both went to extra time in both the first replay and second replays, each three-game tie producing a total playing time of some 430 minutes. John McKay scored the all-important winning goal in the 106th minute of 'Boro's third game against Charlton. The FA Cup match versus Blackpool in 1946 went to a replay after the aggregate score (over two legs) finished level at 5-5.

FIRST PREMIERSHIP GOAL

Brian Deane, who scored 19 goals in 95 games for Middlesbrough between October 1998 and November 2001, having joined the club from Benfica for £3m, holds a record no-one can take away from him. When he was playing for Sheffield United in August 1992, he had the pleasure of netting the first-ever goal in the Premiership against Manchester United at Bramall Lane. He also had the honour of scoring the first goal at Leicester City's Walkers Stadium, in the Foxes' 2-0 win over Watford in August 2002.

TWENTY-ONE DIFFERENT SCORERS

In the 1997/98 season, Middlesbrough scored 93 goals and twenty-one players contributed to that total, including an opponent (Kevin Gray, Huddersfield Town). Mikkel Beck and Paul Merson were joint top scorers with 15 goals each.

BRAZILIAN TRIO

In September 1996, Middlesbrough became the first British club to field three Brazilian footballers in a major Cup competition when Juninho, Emerson and Branco all starred in the 7-0 League Cup victory over Hereford United.

THANK YOU KINDLY

The most own goals received by Middlesbrough in a season of League football is four, 'scored' on five occasions in 1962/63, 1992/93, 2003/04, 2004/05 and 2010/11. In 1962/63, the four own goals were scored in Division Two games by Reeves of Plymouth Argyle when 'Boro won 5-4 at Home Park; by Moore of Derby County in a 3-3 draw at the Baseball Ground; by Wakeman of Charlton Athletic in a 2-1 home victory and by Metcalfe of Norwich City in 'Boro's last 6-2 victory at Ayresome Park. Thirty seasons later, in 1992/93, when 'Boro were playing in the inaugural Premiership season, they received gratuitous 'goals' from Flitcroft (Manchester City), McGrath (Aston Villa), Seaman (Arsenal) and Nicol (Liverpool). 'Boro lost two and drew one of these four games. A decade on, in 2003/04, 'Boro's four gift goals came from Messrs Jihah (Manchester City in a 1-0 win away); Curtis (Leicester City in a 3-3 draw); from Yobo (Everton), in another draw, 1-1 at Goodison Park; and Nolan (Bolton), which set up a 2-0 home win. The very next season, 2004/05, on target for 'Boro were Popović (Crystal Palace), El Karkouri (Charlton Athletic), Purse (West Bromwich Albion) and Higginbottom (Southampton). 'Boro won the first three of these matches by 2-1 and drew 2-2 with Saints at their St Mary's Stadium. And finally in 2010/11, opponents' presents came from Mariappa (Watford), Martin (Norwich City), Cisse (Bristol City) and McCarthy (also of Crystal Palace in the return fixture). 'Boro won one, drew one and lost two of these four matches.

OPPONENTS' PRESENTS

'Boro were gifted a total of six 'goals' in League games in two seasons (1936–38), when opponents put the ball past their own 'keepers. In the first campaign, own goals were scored by James (Brentford), Oakes (Charlton) and Cattlin (Huddersfield), while in the second campaign, opponents on target for 'Boro were Bell (Derby County), Reeday (Leicester City) and Betmead (Grimsby Town). For the record, 'Boro did not lose any of these fixtures. During the first season after the Second World War, in 1946/47, three more players scored 'own goals' to benefit 'Boro: Hughes (Liverpool), Scott (Preston North End) and Forbes (Sheffield United). The first two both gave 'Boro 1-0 wins. Liverpool centre-half Dick White conceded two own goals to give 'Boro a 2-0 home League win in October 1961. Over a period of twenty-five years (1981–2006), four West Bromwich Albion scored 'own goals' against 'Boro: right-back Batson, centre-halves Raven and Purse and midfielder Wallwark, in that order. The unfortunate Purse also conceded an own goal when playing for Sheffield Wednesday against 'Boro in 2009.

INTERNATIONAL 'BORO

This is my choice of 'Boro's best post-Second World War international XI, if they had been with the club at the same time (in a traditional 1-2-3-5 formation, with five named substitutes): Platt; McNeil, Hardwick (captain); Harris, Nurse, Pallister; Mahoney, Mannion, Clough, Peacock, Holliday. Subs: Armstrong, Souness, Crossan, Cochrane, McMordie.

During their respective careers, these sixteen players together amassed a grand total of 301 full caps. Hardwick also starred for Great Britain in 1947, gaining an extra cap.

WEMBLEY VISITS

Middlesbrough have appeared in a senior Cup final at Wembley (at the old and new stadiums) on four occasions, drawing once and losing on three other occasions. In March 1990, they lost 1-0 to Chelsea in the final of the Zenith Data Systems Cup in front of 76,369 fans, and seven years later, in April 1997, when the turn out was 76,757, they drew 1-1 after extra-time with Leicester City in the Coca-Cola-sponsored League Cup final, only to lose the replay 1-0 at Hillsborough.

The very next month, Middlesbrough reached their first-ever FA Cup final, but despite a gutsy performance, and with an audience of 79,160 spectators inside the stadium, they lost 2-0, again to Chelsea, for whom Italian midfielder Roberto Di Matteo scored as early as the 47th second.

Twelve months later, in March 1998, 'Boro played in their second successive Coca Cola League Cup final and disappointingly for all concerned, they were once again thwarted by their now seemingly bogey team. Chelsea registered another 2-0 victory, this time after extra-time, watched live by 77,698 supporters.

In February 2004, with Wembley being rebuilt, Middlesbrough claimed their first major trophy when they beat Bolton Wanderers 2-1 in the Carling League Cup final before a crowd of 72,634 at the Millennium Stadium in Cardiff.

BARE IT ALL

In December 1999, as part of a bet, former Middlesbrough striker Bernie Slaven said, live on a radio station, that he would 'bare his backside' in the shop window of a large department store if 'Boro were to beat Manchester United in a Premiership game at Old Trafford. Amazingly, 'Boro went out and beat second-placed United 3-2 in front of more than 55,000 fans and Slaven duly did what he had promised. He chose the Binns store in the town centre to bare his posterior, with the scoreline written on his buttocks.

WELSH DRAGONS

Surprisingly, few players born in Wales have appeared in first-class matches for Middlesbrough. These are some of the Red Dragons:

Bob Atherton (a native of Bethesda), Clayton Blackmore (Neath), Danny Coyne (Prestatyn), Arthur Davies (Bodhowell), Andy Dibble (Cwmbran), Tom Griffiths (Moss near Wrexham), Bill Harris (Swansea), Joe Hiller (Bridgend), John Love Jones (Rhyl), Ben Lewis (Saltney near Chester), John Mahoney (Cardiff), Mel Nurse (Swansea), Bryan Orritt (Caernarfon), Martin Thomas (Senghenydd), Ernie Walley (Caernarfon), Jesse Tom Williams (Cefn-y-Bedd) and Dick Wynn (Chester). Atherton (4 caps), Blackmore (1), Davies (1), Griffiths (6), Harris (6), Jones (1), Lewis (2), Mahoney (13), Nurse (3) and Warren (3) all won full caps for the Principality as 'Boro players.

Blackmore won a total of 39 caps; his other 38 came with Manchester United. Griffiths claimed 21 overall; Lewis 10 in the 1890s; Mahoney gained 51; Nurse 12 and Warren 6. Lewis won his 2 caps *v.* England and Scotland as early as 1893.

Rhys Williams was born in Australia, for whom he won one full cap before going on to play in ten U21 internationals for Wales. Goalkeeper Mark Crossley was born in Barnsley, but through family connections went on to win eight caps for Wales.

'BORO HAMMERED BY 'BORO!

Middlesbrough claimed their biggest win in the FA Cup way back in October 1890 when they hammered hapless Scarborough 11-0 at home in a qualifying round tie in front of 2,000 loyal supporters. Johnston (3), Wilson, Allen, Petrie (2), Dennis (3) and Stevenson scored the goals against mediocre opposition.

FROM A PORSCHE TO A PRISON

Striker Marlon King, who netted twice in 13 League goals when on loan at Middlesbrough in season 2008/09, was jailed for eighteen months for dangerous driving in May 2014. A year earlier, in April 2013, he was involved in a three-car crash while eating an ice cream as he drove his Porsche Panamera along the A46 in Winthorpe near Newark in Nottinghamshire. The crash left a thirty-five-year-old motorist with a broken arm. He had to be air-lifted to hospital. King had initially pleaded guilty to a charge of dangerous driving at Nottingham Crown Court, and sentencing him to a term of imprisonment, Recorder Paul Mann QC said: 'I do not regard your case as merely impulsive or silly behaviour. It was aggressive. It was arrogant.' King also received a three-year driving ban.

Since 2000, King has had numerous convictions for various offences, most of them relating to cars and motoring. He has received numerous fines, driving bans, community service sentences, a rehabilitation order and was told to pay compensation on convictions, including theft from a person and from a car, criminal damage, and attempting to obtain property by deception; fraudulent use of vehicle licence documents; driving without insurance; speeding; drunk driving; a wounding incident while playing amateur football, and two cases involving assaults of young women rejecting his advances in the Soho area of London.

Three cases led to imprisonment. In May 2002, he received an eighteen-month prison sentence for receiving stolen goods, in relation to a BMW convertible that he was found driving. He was found not guilty of a charge of assaulting a police officer in a related case. His solicitor said, 'Marlon's reputation will be tarnished forever; whatever success he achieves, he'll always be referred to in a Tyson-esque way as someone who has had a criminal past and that is a considerable penalty.' His club, Gillingham, continued to pay his salary while he was in jail, and supported his appeal, which resulted in the sentence being reduced to nine months, with King being released on licence after five months, returning to the Gills within two days of his release.

In December 2008, again in the Soho area, King was arrested on suspicion of punching a twenty-year-old female university student in the face, causing a broken nose and split lip, for which she was treated in hospital. He was later convicted of sexual assault and assault occasioning actual bodily harm, and was sentenced to eighteen months in prison and placed on the Sex Offender Register for seven years. His club, Wigan Athletic, immediately initiated the cancellation of his contract. King's agent at that time, Tony Finnigan, said he was confident that his client would find a club on his release and accused the Professional Footballers' Association (PFA) of failing to offer support. Gordon Taylor, the Chief Executive of the PFA, said that the PFA did not represent players when they have broken the law and been convicted on non-footballing matters. It would support members with anger management or other issues if approached but no approach had been made by King.

After his release, King made an unsuccessful appeal against the conviction.

Since starting his football career in 1998, King, besides his spell with 'Boro', has also played for Barnet, Gillingham, Nottingham Forest, Leeds United, Watford, Wigan Athletic, Hull City, Coventry City, Birmingham City and Sheffield United in that order. At May 2014, his record stood at 167 goals in 500 League and Cup games.

MONEY, MONEY, MONEY

Here are the details of how Middlesbrough's home gate receipts record has been broken over the last fifty years:

£8,175	*v.* Newcastle Utd	FA Cup	December 1964
£8,555	*v.* Peterborough U	Football League	May 1967
£8,946	*v.* Oxford United	Football League	May 1967
£15,755	*v.* Manchester Utd	FA Cup	February 1970
£17,408	*v.* Manchester Utd	FA Cup	January 1972
£24,621	*v.* Sunderland	FA Cup	January 1975
£29,491	*v.* Manchester City	League Cup s/fl	January 1976
£29,982	*v.* Sunderland	League Cup	September 1977
£57,710	*v.* Barnsley	FA Cup	February 1981
£82,835	*v.* Everton	FA Cup	February 1988
£102,530	*v.* Notts County	Div. 2 play-off s/f	May 1991
£178,977	*v.* Manchester Utd	League Cup s/f	March 1992
£200,351	*v.* Newcastle Utd	League Cup	October 1992
£353,549	*v.* Newcastle Utd	League Cup	November 1996
£361,444	*v.* Liverpool	League Cup	February 1998
£486,229	*v.* Newcastle Utd	Premier League	December 1998
£510,000*	*v.* Newcastle Utd	Premier League	March 2003
£534,500*	*v.* Manchester Utd	Premier League	May 2009

*Unofficial figures

FIRST 'BOSMAN' SIGNING

In 1996, Danish striker Mickkel Beck became the first player signed by Middlesbrough under the 'Bosman rule' when he moved to Ayresome Park from the German Bundesliga club Fortuna Cologne.

LEAGUE CUP ROMP

Middlesbrough recorded their biggest League Cup win in September 1996 when they brushed aside Hereford United 7-0 at Ayresome Park in a second-round, first-leg encounter in front of 17,136 spectators. Fleming, Branco, Emerson and Ravanelli (with a four-timer), scored the goals to see off the Bulls.

OFFSIDE LAW: FIRST SEASON

The first season of the current offside (which means that two opponents must be between an opposing player and the goal-line) was introduced for the 1925/26 season, and Middlesbrough, as a team, adapted to it exceedingly well. In their first game under the new rule, 'Boro whipped Portsmouth 5-1 at Fratton Park and quickly followed up with ten more goals in their next three games, beating Blackpool 3-2 (home), Wolverhampton Wanderers 4-1 (home) and Blackpool in the return fixture 3-1 (away). As the season progressed, so the goals continued to flow and after 42 League games and two FA Cup ties had been completed, Middlesbrough finished up with a grand total of 84 while at that same time they conceded 73. This gave a grand total of 157 scored by 'Boro and their opponents in 44 competitive matches, giving an average of almost 3.6 goals per 90 minutes of football. Barrel-chested Scot Jimmy McClelland top scored for 'Boro with 38 goals, 32 in the League and 6 in the FA Cup, 5 coming in an emphatic 5-1 victory over Leeds United in the third round.

REGULAR SQUAD

Middlesbrough manager Bruce Rioch used only eighteen players during the 1987/88 League programme, having utilised nineteen the previous season. Five players (goalkeeper Stephen Pears, defenders Colin Cooper, centre-back Tony Mowbray and Gary Parkinson, along with striker and top-scorer Bernie Slaven) were all ever-presents in 1986/87, while Mowbray, Slaven and Gary Pallister played in every game the following season. Rioch fielded twenty-one players in 1988/89.

NO MEAN RIVALS

This is Middlesbrough's full playing record in the Football League, Premiership, FA Cup, Football League Cup and intermediate competitions, against arch-rivals Newcastle United and Sunderland.

Team	P	W	D	L	F	A
Newcastle United	127	40	38	49	156	185
Sunderland	143	46	37	60	184	207

'Boro first met Newcastle at competitive level on 1 January 1893, when they beat the Magpies 3-2 in a 1st round FA Cup tie at St James' Park in front of 5,000 fans.

Middlesbrough and Sunderland first confronted each other in an FA Cup third qualifying round tie on 26 November 1887. Sunderland led 2-0 at Linthorpe Road before 'Boro pegged them back to 2-2. Then in the replay it was 'Boro who squandered a two-goal lead, eventually losing 4-2. However, the FA subsequently disqualified Sunderland from the competition for fielding three Scots who were all said to be professionals.

BUSY SEASON

Middlesbrough played a record 64 competitive first team games in the 2005/06 season. They competed thirty-eight Premiership matches, in eight FA Cup games, three League Cup ties and fifteen UEFA Cup encounters. 'Boro won 26, drew 14 and lost 24 of these fixtures, scoring 85 goals and conceding 81.

RUMBLED BY ROVERS

Middlesbrough's heaviest defeat in League football came at Ewood Park on 6 November 1954, when they were battered (and bruised) by Blackburn Rovers to the tune of 9-0 in a Second Division match in front of 29,189 spectators. Johnny Quigley and Francis Mooney both scored hat-tricks for rampant Rovers.

WATCH IT, MATE!

Derwick Ormond Goodfellow, an ex-marine commando, was a 6-foot-1-inch-tall goalkeeper with Middlesbrough in the 1940s. Fearing no one, he once picked up the Manchester City centre-forward Eddie McMorran by the throat and placed him back on his feet near the penalty spot, advising him not to come closer to the goal that that.

THIRD MAN

Former Middlesbrough wing-half Jimmy Gordon, who made 253 first-class appearances for the club over a period of eight years between 1946 and 1954, became the third and unsung hero of the Clough-Taylor management team at Derby County, Leeds United (albeit briefly) and Nottingham Forest. He actually led Forest out at Wembley for the 1980 League Cup final against Wolves.

100 UP

Middlesbrough have so far played 100 or more competitive games against seventeen different clubs, as listed here:

Team	Games
Arsenal	129
Aston Villa	139
Birmingham	107
Blackburn Rovers	127
Bolton Wanderers	121
Charlton Athletic	100
Chelsea	114
Derby County	138
Everton	119
Liverpool	141
Manchester City	125

Manchester Utd	123
Newcastle Utd	127
Portsmouth	111
Sheffield Utd	101
Sheffield Wed.	102
Sunderland	143

'Boro have played 90 or more games against Leeds United, Leicester City, Preston, Stoke City, Tottenham and West Bromwich Albion at May 2014.

GLOBETROTTERS

Middlesbrough have so far played competitive football in seventeen different countries: Austria, Belarus, Bulgaria, Czech Republic, England, Germany, Greece, Holland, Italy, Portugal, Romania, Scotland, Serbia, Spain, Switzerland, Ukraine and Wales.

SHORT SPELL

Scottish-born wing-half Tom Doig's 'playing career' with Middlesbrough lasted just three weeks. He made his League debut for the club in a 3-1 home win over Blackpool on 1 December 1900. He played in the next three games against Small Heath and Grimsby Town in the League and against Bishop Auckland in an FA Cup qualifying tie before losing his place in the team to new signing David Smith.

'ROARY' THE LION

Middlesbrough's official mascot is named 'Roary' the Lion and the club runs Roary's Children's Charity Fund, which purchases items for local children's charities.

LONGEST SEASON

Middlesbrough's longest season of competitive football came in 1969/70. It covered nine-and-a-half months from 9 August to 24 May. During that period of time they played fifty-two first-class matches as well as three friendlies. Other long campaigns have been:

> 2008/09 (16 August–24 May); 1999/2000 (7 August–14 May); 1998/98 (15 August–16 May); 2004/05 (14 August–15 May); 1996/97 (17 August–17 May); 2000/01 (19 August–19 May); 2007/08 (11 August–11 May); 2010/11 (7 August–7 May); 2003/04 (16 August–15 May) and 2005/06 (13 August–10 May).

The 1939/40 wartime season ran from 26 August to 5 June (nine months and ten days), during which time 'Boro played only twenty-seven matches.

EARLY START, LATE FINISH

The earliest start Middlesbrough have made to a football season of competitive League and Cup action is 2 August 1975 and the latest day they have ended a campaign was on 21 May 1963. This was due to the Arctic weather conditions that gripped the UK that winter. They also had a late finish at the end of the 1944/45 Second World War season (kicking the last ball also on 21 May) while their activities in 1939/40 ended on 5 June (see *Longest Season,* page 93).

COLD SNAP

Middlesbrough, like every other club in the country, suffered with the Arctic weather conditions that struck the UK in the early part of 1963. Between 30 December 1962 and 9 February 1963 (around six weeks, covering forty-two days), 'Boro did not play a single League or FA Cup game at home or away. In fact, they played only two matches in two and a half months from mid-December. As a result of this lengthy, unscheduled quiet period, the team was forced to complete 12 Second Division games during the last eight weeks of the season (6 April–21 May). And they did rather well, winning even and drawing four. They rose to fourth in the table, missing promotion by only 4 points. Stoke City (champions), Chelsea and Sunderland finished above them.

'Boro rounded of the season with a resounding 6-2 victory over Norwich City at Ayresome Park. This was their best home League win in terms of goals scored since September 1959.

HIGHLY HONOURED

Seven footballers who have been associated with Middlesbrough received a distinction from HRH Queen Elizabeth II. They are Brian Clough (player), Jack Charlton (manager), Bryan Robson (player-manager) and Gordon Strachan (manager) who all received an OBE. Players Viv Anderson, Harold Shepherdson (also assistant-trainer/trainer) and Nobby Stiles were awarded the MBE. Jack Clough, a goalkeeper with 'Boro in the early 1920s, won a Military Medal and Bar as a stretcher bearer during the Second World War.

CRICKET GROUND FIRST!

Linthorpe Road, where 'Boro played several games between 1899 and 1903, was the northern half of a cricket ground. And some years earlier, in July 1882, a three-day match was played there between Yorkshire and the touring Australians. The Aussies won by seven wickets, scoring 222 and 49-3 against Yorkshire's 129 and 140.

ON RECORD

'Boro's other former home, Ayresome Park, is mentioned in the 35th edition of the *Guinness Book of Records* – not for football, but for featuring the largest reported advertising hoarding, which was painted on the roof of the North Stand by sponsor Heritage Hampers.

ST VALENTINE'S DAY MASSACRE

On 14 February 1931, Middlesbrough travelled to Newcastle United for a First Division League game and in front of 31,945 spectators, they 'massacred' the Magpies to the tune of 5-0. George Camsell (2), Welsh international outside-left Fred Warren, his inside partner Kenny Cameron and former Celtic player Johnny 'Jock' McKay scored for rampant 'Boro, who thus completed the double over their rivals, having won 3-1 at Ayresome Park earlier in the season, when Camsell and McKay were also on the score sheet.

NEWCASTLE CONNECTION

Among the many players who, over the years, have represented both Middlesbrough and North East neighbours Newcastle United, we have: Bill Agnew, Andrew Aitken, 'Sam' Ameobi, Stan Anderson, Alum Armstrong, Billy Askew, Ian Baird, Simon Beaton, Ralph Birkett, Joe Blackett, Stuart Boam, Jack Brownlie, Micky Burns, Bob Corbett, John Craggs, Jim Crawford, Dave Cumming (Second World War guest), Billy Day, Andy Donaldson, Chris Duffy, Kieron Dyer, Alan Foggon, Paul Gascoigne, Geremi, Robert Gibson, Jimmy Gordon, John Harris, Pat Heard, John Hendrie, Bill 'Sandy' Higgins, Arthur Horsfield, Peter Johnson, Tom Lamb, Harry Leonard, Alex McCulloch, Alf Maitland, David Mills, Irving Nattaess, Tom Nibloe, Jack Ostler, Ray Parkin, Dick Roberts, Joe Scott, George Smith, goalkeeper Martin Thomas, Norman Thompson, Jim Tyldesley, Tommy Urwin, Mark Viduka, Charlie Wayman, Derek Weddle, Jonathan Woodgate and Micky Young.

Several other United players guested for 'Boro during the Second World War, among them Len Hubble, Laurence Nevins, Ron Sales, Jim Sloan and John Yeats, while Wally Boyes, Allenby Chilton, Alex Herd, Cecil McCormack, Jimmy Mullen, Bill Nicholson, Fred Osborne, Stan Pearson, Sid Peppitt, John Short and John Sphuler all played as guests for both 'Boro and Newcastle (from other clubs) during the Second World War.

George Martin played for Middlesbrough and later managed Newcastle (1947–50), as did Graeme Souness, who was in charge at St James Park from 2004–06. Jack Charlton managed both 'Boro (1973–77) and Newcastle (1984) and Sir Bobby Robson, an amateur player with Middlesbrough (1948), bossed Newcastle (1999–2004). Ex-Sunderland forward Ray Hankin, after retiring, became Newcastle United's Football in the Community Officer.

Irving Nattrass transferred from 'Boro to Newcastle United for a record fee of £475,000 in August 1979.

SAVE OUR STEEL

In 2009, local steel producer Corus Group announced the possibility that it would mothball its Teesside plant, with up to 4,000 employees and contractors facing redundancy, after a consortium of steel magnates walked away from a ten-year deal. Middlesbrough FC helped with the Save Our Steel campaign by hosting dozens of steelworkers and their families as they marched around the ground, promoting the campaign via the stadium's PA system, scoreboards and in match day programmes, while players wore t-shirts during warm-ups promoting the campaign. Chairman Steve Gibson said,

Middlesbrough Football Club exists for the community, for the people of Teesside – and the closure of the steel plants threatens to rip the heart out of our community. We cannot stand by and allow that to happen. We want the steelworkers and their families to know that we are behind them and will help their campaign in any way we can ... We like to think that the football club is the flagship of Teesside. Well this is our town and these are our people and we have to do what we can to help them.

MR CONSISTENCY

David 'Spike' Armstrong made a club record 305 consecutive League appearances for Middlesbrough between Match 1972 and August 1980. In all competitions, his unbroken run stretched to 358 games. He was, of course, an ever-present seven seasons on the trot.

FIVE UP!

Excluding Second World War fixtures, Middlesbrough played five games in a season against the same club on six different occasions. In 1938/39, they played Bolton Wanderers twice in the First Division and three times in the FA Cup. In 1949/50, 'Boro played the same set of matches versus Aston Villa, while in 1964/65 they met Charlton Athletic twice in Division Two, twice in the FA Cup and once in the League Cup. In 1966/67, 'Boro battled against York City in three FA Cup matches and in two League Cup games and followed up the next season by playing Hull City twice in Division Two and three times in the third round of the FA Cup. The last time 'Boro competed against the same opponent five times in the same season was in 1977/78, when they met Everton twice in the First Division, twice in the League Cup and once in the FA Cup.

CHRISTMAS DAY ACTION

Middlesbrough have played thirty League games and five Second World War matches on Christmas Day, their first in 1905 againstBirmingham at home, won 1-0; their last away at Huddersfield Town in 1957, lost 1-0. 'Boro's full record of their 25 December matches is:

Years	P	W	D	L	F	A
1905–57	30	9	9	12	43	62
1940-45	5	4	0	1	17	2
Total	35	13	9	13	60	64

GIFTS AND UNWANTED PRESENTS

'Boro suffered some heavy defeats during Christmas 1909. They were beaten 7-3 at Ayresome Park by Bradford City, crashed 7-1 away to Aston Villa in 1931, were batted 7-1 by Tottenham Hotspur at White Hart Lane in 1952, succumbed to a 5-0 defeat at Leeds in 1936 and were overcome 5-3 by the same team, also at Elland Road in 1937, having lost by the same score at Burnley in 1919.

'Boro's best Christmas Day League wins were 5-3 away at Manchester City in 1926, when George Camsell scored all five goals, and 5-1 at home to Port Vale twelve months later. They also blitzed Bradford City 6-0 at Ayresome Park in 1941 (four goals here for Tommy Dawson) and ran up successive 4-0 home victories over Sunderland in the wartime years of 1942 and 1943.

Despite limited transport facilities, a crowd of 44,077 saw Camsell's five-goal haul at Maine Road in 1926; 43,692 fans attended the game at Roker Park in 1948 and there were 41,318 present at Ayresome Park in 1950.

'Boro contested five goalless draws (out of a total of nine in all) on Christmas Day.

LONG-DISTANCE TRAVELLERS

The longest distance, by road, any Middlesbrough team has had to travel to play a Premiership, Football League or domestic Cup game in England, is 315 miles south to Plymouth Argyle's Home Park ground in Devon. The one-way journey to Torquay is 299 miles; to Exeter it's 281 and to Bournemouth 268, followed by treks of 262 miles to Brighton, 261 to Portsmouth and 253 to Southampton. When 'Boro play in South Wales, they have to travel 228 miles to Cardiff, 233 to Swansea and 276 to Newport and when they met Aberdeen in the Anglo-Scottish Cup in 1975, the trip to Pittodrie Park was 181 miles.

NEUTRAL GROUNDS

Due to various circumstances, laws and regulations, Middlesbrough
have played twenty-two competitive games on a neutral ground:

18 April 1903	*v.* Sunderland (Division One)	lost 1-2	St James' Park	24,887
22 February 1906	*v.* Brighton & HA (FA Cup)	won 3-1	Bramall Lane	11,528
3 February 1930	*v.* Charlton A. (FA Cup)	won 1-0	Maine Road	16,676
4 February 1946	*v.* Blackpool (FA Cup)	won 1-0	Elland Road	29,593
14 September 1946	*v.* Man. Utd (Division One)	lost 0-1	Maine Road	65,279
20 December 1947	*v.* Man. Utd (Division One)	lost 1-2	Maine Road	47,879
2 May 1949	*v.* Man. Utd (Division One)	lost 0-1	Maine Road	22,889
16 January 1950	*v.* Aston Villa (FA Cup)	won 3-0	Elland Road	43,011
16 January 1967	*v.* York City (FA Cup)	won 4-1	St James' Park	21,347
7 February 1968	*v.* Hull City (FA Cup)	won 1-0	Bootham Crescent	16,524
17 January 1976	*v.* Stoke City (Division One)	lost 0-1	Vale Park	21,049
23 August 1986	*v.* Port Vale (Division 3)	drew 2-2	Victoria Ground	3,690
6 April 1997	*v.* Leicester C. (LC final)	drew 1-1	Wembley	76,757
13 April 1997	*v.* Chesterfield (FAC s/f)	drew 3-3	Old Trafford	49,640
16 April 1997	*v.* Leicester C. (LC final rep)	lost 0-1	Hillsborough	39,428
22 April 1997	*v.* Chesterfield (FAC s/f rep)	won 3-0	Hillsborough	30,339
17 May 1997	*v.* Chelsea (FA Cup final)	lost 0-2	Wembley	79,160

28 March 1998	*v.* Chelsea (FL Cup final)	lost 0-2	Wembley	77,698
14 April 2002	*v.* Arsenal (FAC s/f)	lost 0-1	Old Trafford	61,168
29 February 2004	*v.* Bolton Wanderers (LC final)	won 2-1	Millennium Stadium	72,634
23 April 2005	*v.* West Ham U. (FAC s/f)	lost 0-1	Villa Park	39,148
10 May 2005	*v.* Sevilla (UEFA Cup final)	lost 0-4	Eindhoven	30,988

FACT FILE

'Boro played six League games at Maine Road in three seasons: 1946–49. They took on Manchester City three times and Manchester United three times, the latter because Old Trafford had been badly damaged by German bombs at the end of the Second World War.

'Boro played at Vale Park in 1976 because one of the stands at Stoke City's Victoria Ground had suffered heavy storm damage.

Ten years later, 'Boro met Port Vale at Hartlepool United's Victoria Ground for an evening Third Division game, and this after the Football League had temporarily closed Ayresome Park following an Inland revenue investigation.

RICH BOSS

It is believed that Peter McWilliam became the first £1,500-a-year manager when he took charge of Middlesbrough in April 1927. This was regarded as a phenomenal sum of money to pay someone to look after a football team. Unfortunately, McWilliam never really won over the supporters, although he saw 'Boro win the Second Division championship at the end of the 1926/27 season and led them to victory in the same Division in 1928/29, before his sacking in March 1934.

HEAVY FIXTURE LIST ENDS IN GLORY

Between 1 April and 2 May 1992, Middlesbrough,charging towards promotion and a place in the newly formed Premier League, played eleven League games in the space of four and a half weeks, winning six, drawing one and losing four.

They ended this very hectic end-of-season programme on a high by recording a hard-earned and money guaranteed 2-1 victory away to Wolverhampton Wanderers before 19,123 spectators. In fact, this vital encounter was almost postponed due to an arson attack at Molineux, but thankfully (from 'Boro's point of view), it went ahead. Despite having Nicky Mohan sent off, they claimed a stupendous victory courtesy of a scrambled equaliser by Jon Gittens (on loan from Southampton) and the winner from Paul Wilkinson to edge out Derby County (2-1 victors over Swindon Town) by two points to claim their place in the top flight as runners-up to Ipswich Town.

TIGHT SCHEDULES

Middlesbrough played a total of seventeen League games during a period of two months and eight days, from 3 March to 11 May 1979.

Fifteen years later, the team bettered that feat by a whisker when seventeen League games were completed in just over two months between 5 March and 8 May 1994.

'Boro contested 16 League games between 4 March and 16 May 1967; did likewise between 5 March and 14 May 1977; repeated the feat between 3 March and 9 May 1987 and played the same number of matches again in 1992 (see *Heavy Fixture List* page 101).

The club has rounded off a season with fifteen-game sequences on three occasions: 1932/33; some fifty-five years later in 1987/88 (this run included four play-off games); in 1989/90 and likewise in 1994/95.

End-of-season League runs of fourteen matches in around two months have occurred in 1900/01, 1965/66, 1977/78, 1979/80, 1982/83 and 1985/86. 'Boro also played 17 games (13 in the League and 4 in the FA Cup) between 1 March and 17 May 1997 and they repeated this again in 2005/06 with 12 League games and 5 UEFA Cup matches played between 4 March and 10 May.

FOUNDER MEMBERS OF THE PREMIERSHIP

The 1992/93 season saw the first games played in the newly-formed Premiership and these were the twenty-two teams who competed in that inaugural campaign: Arsenal, Aston Villa, Blackburn Rovers, Chelsea, Coventry City, Crystal Palace, Everton, Ipswich Town, Leeds United, Liverpool, Manchester City, Manchester United, Middlesbrough, Norwich City, Nottingham Forest, Oldham Athletic, Queens Park Rangers, Sheffield United, Sheffield Wednesday, Southampton, Tottenham Hotspur and Wimbledon.

Manchester United won the title ahead of Aston Villa, with Norwich third. Unfortunately, 'Boro (who finished twenty-first) were relegated along with Crystal Palace and Nottingham Forest. These teams were replaced by Newcastle United, Swindon Town and West Ham United.

BY GEORGE!

George Camsell hit 59 League goals for Middlesbrough in 1926/27 to become the first player to top the half-century mark in a single season. He was also the first footballer to score 300 League goals for one club (Middlesbrough) whom he served for seventeen years from October 1925 to May 1942. He reached the historic milestone on 6 March 1937 in a 3-2 win over Everton at Goodison Park. Camsell went on to net a total of 345 goals in 453 competitive appearances for 'Boro (325 in the Football League) as well as hitting another 21 in 33 games during the Second World War. And of course he bagged an astonishing eighteen goals in only nine full internationals for England. Some marksman, eh?

'TIM' WILLIAMSON: SUPER 'KEEPER

Goalkeeper Reginald Garnet 'Tim' Williamson holds the record for most appearances for Middlesbrough, a record one feels will never be beaten. Between April 1902 and March 1923, he lined up in 563

League games and 39 FA Cup matches, and played in 14 Northern Victory League games in the wartime season of 1918/19, for an overall total of 616. Beside his record appearance tally, Williamson also managed to score two penalties, in a 2-2 home League draw with Liverpool in April 1910 and in the 3-0 home League victory over Bristol City five months later. He also captained the team on several occasions and played in seven full internationals for England (up to 1913), making his debut against Ireland on his home ground, Ayresome Park, in February 1905, when he unfortunately conceded an own goal in a 1-1 draw.

MISSED 'EM

Bobby Robson (later Sir Bobby, CBE) was an amateur with Middlesbrough in 1948 but was allowed to leave Ayresome Park by manager David Jack. And we all know what happened after that!

Initially an inside-forward and later a right-half, he made a total of 627 senior appearances (585 in the League) playing for just two clubs, Fulham (1950–56 and 1962–67) and West Bromwich Albion (1956–62). He won one 'B', one U23 and 20 full caps for England and played in the 1958 and 1962 World Cups. As a manager/coach, he served Vancouver Royals (Canada), Ipswich Town (1969–82), England (also England 'B'), Dutch club PSV Eindhoven (two spells), Sporting Lisbon and FC Porto, both in Portugal, CF Barcelona and finally Newcastle United (1999–2004), being in charge of his clubs in 1,446 matches at various levels, with almost a 50 per cent win rate. Robson won the FA Cup and UEFA Cup with Ipswich (1978 and 1981), two Dutch League titles with PSV (1991 and 1992), Portugal's Primera League with Porto in 1995 and 1996 and completed the Copa Del Rey, European Cup-Winner's Cup and European Super Cup treble with Barcelona in 1997.

George Campbell Stobbart, born in Morpeth in January 1921, played as an inside or centre-forward for Netherfield before joining Middlesbrough as an eighteen-year-old in May 1939. During the Second World War, he played as a guest for South Shields and Darlington besides scoring 125 goals for 'Boro, but soon after peacetime football had returned, and without ever playing in major Football League or FA Cup games, he was sold to Newcastle United for £4,650 in September 1946. Over the next decade, Stobbart scored at will, netting 22 goals in 72 outings for the Magpies, 35 in 115 for Luton Town (October 1949–August 1952), 32 in 79 for Millwall (up to September 1954) and 19 in 60 for Brentford (up to May 1956). He rounded off his career with Bedford Town, and died in 1995, aged seventy-four.

You win some you lose some, as they say. Top player, top manager, top man.

GYPSY JOE

Goalkeeper Joe Frail, who deputised for Williamson (early 1900s) several times and made sixty-four appearances between the posts for Middlesbrough, was a real gypsy who lived in a caravan during his playing days, which were spent with Burslem Port Vale (1892), Gorton Villa, Glossop North End, Derby County, Chatham, Middlesbrough (1900–02), Luton Town, Brentford, Stalybridge Celtic, Middlesbrough again (1903–05), Stockport County and Glossop for a second time. He always wore a knotted handkerchief round his neck and ran a market stall in Middlesbrough town centre where fans could take penalties against him for fun. He was certainly a good goalkeeper and once saved three spot-kicks in a League game for Brentford. Despite several police convictions for various crimes and misdemeanours against his name, he was a fine goalkeeper, a real character, who was born in Stoke-on-Trent in 1869 and died in 1939, aged seventy.

TEAM COLOURS

When Middlesbrough gained entry into the Football League, they played in white shirts and blue shorts, with a change strip of black shirts and white shorts.

CELEBRITY FANS

Here are some of Boro's celebrity supporters. Most of them have been seen at matches, some even wearing a club shirt:

Singers James Arthur, Bryan Ferry, Alistair Griffiths (Fame Academy), Chris Rea, Paul Rodgers (from the group Free) and rock vocalist Paul Smith (Maximo Park); TV judge and singing star Nicole Scherzinger; comedian Roy 'Chubby' Brown; Channel 4 newsreader Jon Snow; TV presenter Selina Scott; Channel 4 racing expert Derek Thompson; *Guardian* columnist Harry Pearson; *Football365* journalist John Nicholson; ex-referee Jeff Winter; former jockey Bob Champion; Franc Roddam, creator of *Auf Wiedersehen Pet*; the comedy duo of Vic Reeves and Bob Mortimer; ex-players Chris Kamara and Graeme Souness (both still have soft spots for the club); television and radio presenter and stand-up comic Kirsten O'Brien; Yorkshire and England cricketer Liam Plunkett; former MI5 officer David Shayler; renowned French chef Jean Christophe Novelli; actors Mark Benton, Bill Fellows, Richard Griffiths OBE, Jamie Parker and Stephen Tompkinson; actress Preeti Deasai; writer Craig Douglas and Gary Cooper, special effects manager for the film *Charlie and the Chocolate Factory*.

Late in life, British Prime Minister William Gladstone followed the fortunes of Middlesbrough.

CUP DOUBLE

Middlesbrough is the only football club so far to have won both the FA Amateur Cup, doing so twice in 1895 and 1898, and the Football League Cup, lifted in 2004.

'BORO AT WAR

Middlesbrough played only 14 games during the First World War, all of them in the Northern Victory League (11 January–19 April 1919).

However, circumstances were very different in the Second World War when the club fulfilled a total of 255 fixtures over the course of six seasons, 1939/40 to 1945/46 inclusive. This is 'Boro's complete record in wartime football:

Season	P	W	D	L	F	A
1918/19	14	9	2	3	28	12
1939/40	27	9	6	12	59	57
1940/41	33	18	3	12	94	81
1941/42	36	13	7	16	81	92
1942/43	36	9	4	23	61	119
1943/44	39	10	10	19	76	104
1944/45	42	12	5	25	73	115
1945/46	41	17	9	16	75	87
Total	269	97	46	126	547	667

WARTIME LOG

In 1939/40, 'Boro played three League Division One games, the results of which were subsequently declared null and void (due to the outbreak of the war), twenty in the North Eastern Regional League and four in the League North Cup competition.

The following season, 1940/41, 'Boro competed once more in the North Eastern Regional League, playing twenty-four games. They contested six in the League North Cup and another three in the West Riding Cup.

In 1941/42. 1942/43, 1943/44 and 1944/45, 'Boro's commitment was confined to the Football League Northern Section (First and Second Championships) and the Wartime League Cup (qualifying competition), playing in turn totals of 36, 36, 39 and 42 matches.

In the transitional season 1945/46, they played 42 games in the Football League Northern Section, which comprised 22 teams. They are also contested seven matches in the FA Cup but these have not been included in wartime statistics.

There were goals scored in every single game 'Boro played in during seasons 1939/40, 1940/41 and 1941/42.

In 1940/41, the team netted 26 goals in four games against York City and 18 in just two encounters versus Sheffield Wednesday.

York were on the receiving end again in 1941/42 when 'Boro bagged 34 in five meetings with the Minstermen and they also scored 34 in six meetings with rivals Newcastle United.

The following season, 'Boro struck another 32 in six matches *v.* Newcastle and 46 in eight against Sunderland.

'Boro lost eight wartime matches in a row between 31 October and 19 December 1942, conceding 36 goals in the process. Soon afterwards they embarked on another disastrous run, losing ten on the bounce between 16 January and 20 March 1943, giving away 48 goals this time round. In fact, during the 1942/43 campaign, 'Boro lost 20 out of 22 matches they took part in over a period of three and a half months: 31 October to 20 March inclusive. They won the other two.

In 1944/45, the five games involving 'Boro and Darlington produced a total of 25 goals and there were 16 goals scored in the two FL (North) encounters against Sheffield United in 1945/46 and 17 in two versus Huddersfield Town in the same season.

A ten-goal thriller between Gateshead and 'Boro at Redheugh Park in mid-September 1944 ended in a 5-5 draw. Centre-forward George Stobbart scored four for 'Boro's in front of 2,000 hardy supporters.

'BORO'S BIGGEST WINS IN WARTIME FOOTBALL, SIX OR MORE GOALS SCORED

8-0 *v.* Hull City (a), April 1941

8-1 *v.* Darlington (h), December 1939

8-2 *v.* Hartlepool United (h), March 1919

8-2 *v.* Bradford City (h), January 1941

7-1 *v.* Gateshead (h), March 1942

7-2 *v.* Sheffield United (a), January 1946

7-3 *v.* Halifax Town (h), April 1943

6-0 *v.* Bradford City (h), December 1941

6-1 *v.* York City (h), June 1940

6-2 *v.* Hartlepool United (a), April 1944

6-2 *v.* Bradford City (h), October 1940

5-0 *v.* Durham City (h), January 1919

George Elliott scored six goals (a double hat-trick) in the win over Hartlepool in 1919 and George Camsell netted a five-timer during the win at Hull in 1941.

'BORO'S HEAVIEST DEFEATS IN WARTIME FOOTBALL, SIX OR MORE GOALS CONCEDED

5-9 *v.* York City (a), September 1941

0-8 *v.* Darlington (a), March 1940

0-8 *v.* Sunderland (a), March 1943

1-8 *v.* Bradford City (h), October 1943

1-8 *v.* Burnley (a), February 1946

2-8 *v.* Newcastle United (h), October 1944

2-8 *v.* Huddersfield Town (h), October 1945

0-7 *v.* Newcastle United (h), December 1941

0-7 *v.* Sunderland (a), January 1943

0-7 *v.* Huddersfield Town (a), October 1945

2-7 *v.* Sunderland (h), December 1942

3-7 *v.* Newcastle United (h), January 1943

4-7 *v.* Newcastle United (a), December 1941

0-6 *v.* Sunderland (a), December 1941

0-6 *v.* Gateshead (a), January 1943

0-6 *v.* York City (a) February 1943

0-6 *v.* Newcastle United, September 1945

1-6 *v.* Newcastle United (h), November 1942

1-6 *v.* Sunderland (a), December 1943

2-6 *v.* Newcastle United (a), February 1941

2-6 *v.* Darlington (h), September 1943

3-6 *v.* Sheffield Wednesday (a), November 1940

4-6 *v.* Hartlepools United (a), December 1945

4-6 *v.* Darlington (a), February 1945

MIDDLESBROUGH v. NEWCASTLE UNITED IN WARTIME FOOTBALL

This is 'Boro's record against their near neighbours from Tyneside:

Venue	P	W	D	L	F	A
Home	19	6	3	10	37	65
Away	18	3	3	12	24	51
Total	37	9	6	22	61	116

An average of 4.6 goals were scored in each game; Newcastle registered 5-1, 6-1, 7-0, 7-3 and 8-2 wins at Ayresome and 5-1, 6-2 and 7-4 victories at St James Park. 'Boro's biggest wins out their nine were those of 4-1 and 5-3 at home and 5-3 away. Newcastle hit 'Boro for seven in both home and away games in the space of a week in December 1941.

MIDDLESBROUGH v. SUNDERLAND IN WARTIME FOOTBALL

This is 'Boro's record against the Wearsiders from Roker Park:

Venue	P	W	D	L	F	A
Home	15	8	1	6	36	33
Away	15	3	3	9	20	52
Total	30	11	4	15	56	85

The thirty games played produced a total of 141 goals, giving an average of 4.7 per 90 minutes of football action.

Sunderland recorded wins of 5-1, 5-4 and 7-2 at Ayresome and 6-0, 6-1, 7-0 and 8-0 at Roker Park. There was also a 4-4 draw on Sunderland soil.

MIDDLESBROUGH'S TOP TEN WARTIME APPEARANCE-MAKERS

168	George Stobbart
131	Bob Stuart
121	David Cumming
105	Billy Forrest
81	Ray Simpson
76	Tom E. Murphy
75	Micky Fenton
50	Wilf Mannion
47	Bill H. Brown
46	John Towers

MIDDLESBROUGH'S TOP TEN WARTIME GOALSCORERS

125	George Stobbart
63	Micky Fenton
21	George Camsell
20	George Elliott
18	Tommy Dawson
17	Tom Murphy
16	Ray Simpson
14	Billy Forrest
13	Jack Robinson
12	John Sphuler

WARTIME GUESTS

During the seven seasons of Second World War football (1939–46), around 160 guest players turned out for Middlesbrough, with 41 starring in 1944/45, 35 in 1941/42 and 33 in 1942/43.

Among the big-named players who chose to assist 'Boro when on leave or were based in the North East of England, were:

Internationals (or future internationals) Ralph Birkett (Newcastle United), Wally Boyes (Everton), Matt Busby (Liverpool, later manager of Manchester United), Johnny Carey and Allenby Chilton (both of Manchester United), Wilf Copping (Leeds United), Joe Hardisty (Bishop Auckland, famous amateur international), Alex Herd (Manchester City), Harry Kinsell (WBA), Jimmy Mullen (Wolverhampton Wanderers), Bill Nicholson (Tottenham Hotspur), Stan Pearson (Manchester United), Stan Rickaby (South Bank, who would join 'Boro in 1946) and Jackie Robinson (Sheffield Wednesday) plus Frank Baker (Stoke City), Tom Blenkinsopp (Grimsby Town, later to join 'Boro), Tommy Dawson (Charlton Athletic), Jimmy Denmark, future Aston Villa inside-left Johnny Dixon, Len Hubble, Ron Sales, Jim Sloan, John Yeats (all from Newcastle United), Cecil McCormack (Gateshead), David McKerrill (Falkirk), Irving Methley (Walsall), Billy Mould, Alex Ormston and Syd Peppitt (all of Stoke City), Fred Osborne (Aston Villa), inside-left Arthur Rowley (West Bromwich Albion, who went on to become the most prolific scorer in Football League history with 434 goals with WBA, Fulham, Leicester City and Shrewsbury Town), John D Short (Leeds United), John Sphuler (Sunderland, later to sign for 'Boro) and Guy Wharton (FA Cup final winner 1939 with Portsmouth).

FIRST WIN ON THE ROAD

It took Middlesbrough nineteen attempts before they finally registered their first away win in the Football League, doing so on 22 September 1900 at Chesterfield in a Second Division match. A crowd of 4,000 saw 'Jock' Brown (2, 1 a penalty) and Martin Moran score the goals in a 3-2 victory at the Recreation Ground, Saltergate.

TRADEMARK

Two Australians, both named Mark (goalkeeper Schwarzer and forward Viduka) played for Middlesbrough against Sevilla in the 2006 UEFA Cup final defeat in Eindhoven.

PLAYERS ON DUTY

Middlesbrough used a total of thirty-nine players during the 1899/1900 season, including nine different centre-forwards. The fewest number of players used by 'Boro in first-class matches during a complete season is 17 in 1983/84. The club called on the services of 18 players in 1926/27 and 1987/88.

PROFESSIONAL STATUS

Middlesbrough became a professional club on 28 February 1899, under the chairmanship of Mr R.H. Forrester. Professionalism in football had officially come into force four years earlier, at a time when Middlesbrough were one of the leading amateur teams in the country, winning the FA Amateur Cup twice in three years: 1895 and 1898.

PLASTIC PITCH

On the 2 January 1982, Queens Park Rangers and Middlesbrough met in the third round of the FA Cup at Loftus Road. This was the first game in the competition ever to be played on an all-weather/plastic/artificial surface. A crowd of 12,100 witnessed the 1-1 draw before QPR won the replay (on grass at Ayresome Park), 3-2 after extra-time.

OWN GOAL DISMAY

The first goalkeeper to give away an own goal in a full international match was Tim Williamson of Middlesbrough, who conceded playing for England against Ireland in February 1905, and on his own ground, Ayresome Park, of all places. The game ended in a 1-1 draw.

NEAR NEIGHBOURS

As the crow flies, Hartlepool United is the nearest Football League club to Middlesbrough, barely 7 miles away (11.26 km).

ON HOME SOIL

Middlesbrough have officially played home games at the following venues: Old Archery Ground (1877–79); Breckon Hill Road (1879–82); Linthorpe Road (1882–1903); Ayresome Park (1903–95); Victoria Park (1986) and the Riverside Stadium (1995–present).

'Boro spent two seasons playing on the Old Archery Ground in Albert Park. They spent the next three (from March 1879) at Breckon Hill Road, a field that they rented from a Mr Kemp, before establishing themselves at Linthorpe Road, which was officially 'opened' for football matches in 1880. The facilities at that time comprised a grandstand (sited on the north side) and narrow open seating around the touchlines with certain amount of room for standing spectators. There were a few odd outbuildings located on the east side, which were used as dressing rooms and refreshment areas. 'Boro played sixty-eight League games at Linthorpe Park, where the biggest crowd was 17,000 against Everton in September 1902.

Ayresome Park cost £11,000 to build and had an initial capacity of 40,000 in 1903. As time passed by this rose steadily, leading to a record turnout of 53,802 for the First Division League game against Newcastle United on 27 December 1949. 'Boro played 1,689 League games at this ground (including three Play-offs) and in 1966 three

Group 4 World Cup finals matches were staged there, all involving North Korea, who, in fact, became the first Asian country to win a Group game in a World Cup tournament when they beat Italy 1-0. Three England internationals were also played at the 'Park' (1905 *v.* Ireland, 1914 *v.* Ireland and 1937 *v.* Wales). When 'Boro moved out in 1995 the ground was demolished.

With the club in severe financial difficulties, 'Boro were not allowed to use Ayresome Park at the start of the 1986/87 season, and therefore played Port Vale at Hartlepool United's Victoria Park ground on 23 August, drawing 2-2 in a Third Division game in front of 3,690 spectators.

Officially opened for 'action' in August 1995 and initially called the BT Cellnet Riverside Stadium, 'Boro's current home ground was constructed on the site of the Yorkshire Tube Works as part of an urban regeneration scheme. There were several problems involved with building the stadium, mainly caused by its location. One problem was that the surveyors thought that there might be Anthrax spores buried beneath the ground. There were also safety issues concerning the gasses being produced in factories in the surrounding area. However, the go ahead was given to build and when complete, it had a continuous cantilever roof covering three single-tier stands and a two-tier cantilever roofed stand on the west side, giving an all-seated capacity of 29,977. Further stands were subsequently constructed in the north-west and south-west corners (thus enclosing the stadium) and by 2002 the capacity had risen to 35,100. It has since been reduced to 34,998.

Up to May 2014, the biggest recorded crowd at the 'Riverside' has been 34,836 *v.* Norwich City in the Premiership on 28 December 2004. The lowest turnout to date was 3,918 *v.* Northampton Town, League Cup, on 11 September 2001.

'Boro have now played 385 home League games at the Riverside Stadium; the first was against Chelsea in 1995 (won 2-0) before a crowd of 28,286, the latest *v.* Barnsley on 26 April 2014 (won 2-1).

'BORO PLAYERS AT WORLD CUPS

The following fifteen players were chosen to represent their country at the World Cup finals while contracted to 'Boro:

1950 Wilf Mannion (England); 1962 Alan Peacock (England); 1982 Jim Platt (Northern Ireland); 1900 Bernie Slaven (Ireland); 1994 Jaime Moreno (Bolivia); 1998 Paul Merson (England) and Hamilton Ricard (Columbia); 2002 Alan Bokšić (FSR Yugoslavia) and Juninho (Brazil); 2006 Stewart Downing (England) and Mark Schwarzer and Mark Viduka (Australia); 2010 Chris Killen (New Zealand); and 2014 Albert Adomah (Ghana) and Kenneth Omeruo (Nigeria).

Future 'Boro player/manager Bryan Robson scored the fourth fastest goal in World Cup final history, netting after just 27 seconds for England against France in Spain 1982.

FIRST TIE, FIRST DEFEAT, FIRST WIN

Unfortunately, 'Boro didn't fare too well in their very first FA Cup game, losing 5-1 at home to Staveley, a Derbyshire mining side, in a bruising first-round encounter on 10 November 1883. Archie Pringle scored the club's first goal in this competition before 1,500 spectators at Linthorpe Road. Just over a year later, Pringle struck twice when 'Boro claimed their first win in the FA Cup competition, defeating Newark (Notts) 4-1 at home on 6 December 1884. They received a bye in the next round but were then dumped out of the competition by six-time finalists and twice winners of the trophy, Old Etonians, 5-2 in round 4.

DON'T FORGET YOUR BOOTS!

Centre-half Jack Dent was selected to play for 'Boro in an away Second World War League North Cup fixture against Huddersfield Town in February 1943. He was not on the phone, and with no emails available, the only way the club could let him know was by sending him a postcard. Dent got the card on the morning of the game, from the 'Boro manager Wilf Gillow. Besides stating where he had to meet the team coach, it also said, 'Bring your own football boots.'

UNUSUAL NAMES

Over the years, Middlesbrough have recruited several players with very unusual Christian names ... names you would never give your child today, or would you? Here are a few (not including overseas signings or players born into a foreign background):

William Barbour Agnew, Walter Bottomley Auld, Raymond Scholey Barnard, George Washington Elliott, George Heads Emmerson, John Proctor French, William Lazenby Gates, Berthold Couldwell Hall, George Moutry Hardwick, John Love Jones, Brian Athol Jordan, Harry Droxford Leonard, Alex Bryce Linwood, Don Sanderson Masson, Esmond Million, Keith Padre O'Neill, Fred Pentland Beaconsfield, Emor Ratcliffe, Joe Cumpson Scott, Michael Lauriston Thomas, James Clabby Townsend, Don 'Hunter' Walker, William Murdoch Morrison Whigham, Reginald Garnet ('Tiny') Williamson, Andrew Nesbit Wilson and Ben Collard Yorston.

DOWN IN WALES

Middlesbrough needed only a draw at Cardiff in their forty-second and final League game of the 1965/66 season to avoid being demoted to the Third Division. For only the second time that term, they scored three goals on the road, but the Welsh club netted five in reply and that meant relegation for Raich Carter's men after a 5-3 defeat.

WHISTFUL SINGING

At 11.20 p.m. on 21 December 1935, having just played a game of whist in a Birmingham club, outside-left Arthur Cunliffe was signed by Middlesbrough from Aston Villa for £8,000. The following day Cunliffe joined up with his new team-mates for a League game against Portsmouth at Fratton Park. Unfortunately, it wasn't a happy start for the winger, as Pompey won the game 1-0.

'BORO'S FIRST STAR PLAYER

Local-born centre-forward Billy Pickstock was Middlesbrough's first star player. He was registered with the club between 1877 and 1880 and scored over 100 goals against a variety of teams. He was a huge favourite with the supporters and could well have become a film star had not he chosen to kick a ball around instead. After retiring from the game he became a very supportive committee member.

UNFINISHED BUSINESS

Seven games involving Middlesbrough have been abandoned for various reasons. They are ('Boro's score given first):

Football League

25 December 1912	v. Bradford C (a)	0-1	84 mins (poor light)	'Boro won replay 2-1
3 April 1953	v. Oldham A (a)	4-1	56 mins (injury)	Result stood
4 December 1922	v. Everton (a)	0-1	57 mins (snow)	'Boro lost replay 4-1
16 November 1929	v. Arsenal (a)	0-1	55 mins (fog)	'Boro won replay 2-1
24 September 1974	v. Leicester City (h)	1-0	29 mins (no lights)	'Boro won replay 3-0

FA Cup

10 January 1959	v. Birmingham City (h)	1-1	60 mins (icy pitch)	'Boro lost 1-0

Floodlit Friendly

12 May 1960	v. Bonn (a)	1-1	74 mins (storm)	Result stood

The game in 1915 was abandoned when Oldham defender Billy Cook refused to leave the field after being sent off. The score was allowed to stand as the final result. And the game against Leicester in 1974 was called off when the Ayresome Park floodlights failed.

The friendly against Bonn in 1960 was called off due to a wicked thunderstorm.

BLOW IT AGAIN, SAM!

In the 1989/90 season, 'Boro's manager Bruce Rioch introduced a number of measures to clean up the chanting and encourage supporters to get behind the team. He engaged a bugler to play various tunes before kick-off to get the fans in the mood.

LIGHTS ON

Floodlights were installed for the first time at 'Boro's Ayresome Park ground in 1957 and the first visiting team to play under the new system was Sunderland on 16 October of that year. A crowd of 27,273 attended the big 'switch on' to watch 'Boro win 2-0 with goals from Brian Clough and Arthur Fitzsimons. A fortnight later, 'Boro beat Newcastle United 3-0 in a second floodlit friendly and followed up later in the season by beating Celtic 6-1 (four goals here for Clough), drawing 3-3 with the Dutch club PSV Eindhoven and losing 2-1 to German side FC Cologne and 5-0 to another Scottish League team, Hibernian.

FIRST GOAL IN TOP FLIGHT

Alex 'Sandy' Robertson had the honour and pleasure of scoring Middlesbrough's first goal in top flight football. It proved to be the winner away at Blackburn Rovers on 1 September 1902. Robertson then netted the club's first home Division One goal in the very next match to beat Everton 1-0.

TURN UP THE RADIO

Radio Ayresome went live on air at the start of the 1966/67 season and was hosted by Bernard Gent from a studio in the South Terrace. Bernard will be fondly remembered for introducing 'Boro's well known run-out theme, 'The Power Game', which greeted the players onto the pitch for nearly thirty years.

LAST GAME DOWN THE ROAD

Middlesbrough's last first-class game at Linthorpe Road was against Stoke on 25 April 1903. A crowd of 10,000 saw David Currie score the club's final League goal in a 1-1 draw with Aston Villa.

NICKNAMES

It is a known fact that most footballers end up with a nickname, given to them by the fans or their colleagues. Here are a few Middlesbrough players with 'extra' names. The date given is in most cases, the first year the player was with the club:

Andrew 'Daller' Aitken (1906), Viv 'Spider' Anderson (1994), David 'Spike' Armstrong (1970s), Jimmy 'Daisy' Bell (1905), William 'Nobby' Bell (1899), Clayton 'Sunbed' Blackmore (1994), Steve 'Paleface' Bloomer (1905), Mark 'Brenda' Brennan (1989), Peter 'Salty' Brine (1970s), Alex 'Sandy' Brown (1900), John 'Jock' Brown (1900), Jack 'Snake Hips' Brownlie (1982), Mark 'Sooty' Burke (1987), Harry 'Pep' Carr (1910), Willie 'Puddin' Carr (1910), Cliff 'The Poacher' Chadwick (1930s), Alex 'Sandy' Cochrane (1922), Ernest 'Tim' Coleman (1934), David 'Kid' Currie (1982), Lloyd 'Lindy' Delaphena (1950), Percival 'Peter' Dickinson (1924), Ugochuku 'Ugo' Ehiogu (2000), Edmund 'Ninty' Eyre (1911), Alan 'The Flying Pig' Foggon (1972), Tom 'Duck' Freeman (1932), Jack 'Carnera' French (1924, after the famous boxer, Primo), Dean 'Dino' Glover (1987), Billy 'Snip' Godley (1903), Jerrel 'Jimmy Floyd' Hasselbaink (2004), John 'Hicky' Hickton (1960s/70s), Bill 'Sandy' Higgins (1900), 'Gentleman

Joe' Hisbent (1911), Ernest 'Joe' Hillier (1929), David 'Hodgy' Hodgson (1978), Walter 'Squire' Holmes (1914), 'Gentleman Jim' Howie (1921), Abraham 'Bullet' Jones (1901), Arthur 'Danny' Kaye (1960), George 'Foo' Kinnell (1968), Dick 'Flip' Le Flem (1964), John 'Jean' McFarlane (1929), John 'Jock' McKay (1926), Peter 'Ma Ba' McKennan (1949), Alex 'Eric' McMordie (1964), Alex 'Alan' McNeill (1967), Albert 'Happy' Nelmes (1890s), Bryan 'Taffy' Orritt (1962), Hendrikus 'Heine' Otto (1981), Andy 'The Padiham Predator' Payton (1991), Emanuel 'Manny' Pogatetz (2005), Alonzo 'Jerry' Poulton (1919), Emor 'Jack' Ratcliffe (1905), Alex 'Sandy' Robertson (1900), Bryan 'Pop' Robson (1994), Robert 'Rab' Shannon (1991), Bernie 'The Wolfman' Slaven (1985), Ernest 'Bert' Smith (1923), Norbert 'Nobby' Stiles (1971), Willie 'Rubber' Thompson (1905), Walter 'One-a-week' Tinsley (1913), Şanli 'Brave Heart' Tuncay (2007), Ted 'Fishy' Verrill (1907), Bob 'Blue' Wanless (1899), Alex 'Sandy' Wardrope (1910), Reginald 'Tiny' Williamson (1901), Jimmy 'The Wizard' Windridge (1911), Archie 'Baldy' Wilson (1914) and Boudewijn 'Bolo' Zenden (2003).

We also have Billy 'The Bear of Bruges' Ashcroft and 'Sir' Bob Baxter (to the younger players). In the 1970s, Stuart Boam and Willie Maddren were the 'telescopic twins'. Ronnie Dicks was the 'handyman of Ayresome Park', said his manager David Jack. Curtis Fleming was the 'Black Pearl of Inchicore', Mark II (Paul McGrath was Mark I). Jaime Moreno was 'Il Pichon' (the roadrunner), Ray Parlour was 'The Romford Pele' and Andy Wilson ('Boro: 1914/23) was called the 'Babe Ruth of Soccer' after he had scored 62 goals playing for Scotland on tour in Canada and the USA in the 1920s. Years ago the whole Middlesbrough team was referred to as the 'Scabs' when they played local rivals Ironopolis, who were known as the 'Washers' or the 'Nops'.

Several players who were initially christened Henry were often called Harry, John became Jack/Jackie and invariably Patrick (especially if he was born in Ireland) is a Paddy, anyone from Scotland is called Jock while a Welshman could be Dai.

FOUR GAMES IN EIGHT DAYS

After losing their first two Second Division League games at Lincoln and Port Vale on 2 and 4 September 1899, Middlesbrough beat

Kaffirs 8-2 in a home friendly on the seventh of the month in front of 3,000 spectators before losing a third League game at home to Small Heath by 3-1 on 9 September. It was certainly a hectic period for the team; in fact during that month of September, 'Boro fulfilled seven matches.

SCHOOL PALS

Middlesbrough Chairman Steve Gibson and 1993 midfielder Chris Kamara went to the same school together on Park End Estate. Kamara went on to have a long career, spanning twenty years (1975–95). He is now a football pundit on Sky Sports.

THREE FA CUP SEMI-FINALS

So far Middlesbrough have reached the semi-final stage of the FA Cup on three separate occasions, in 1997, 2002 and 2006. They won the first one to reach the final but lost the last two, both by a goal to nil.

In season 1996/97, after knocking out Chester 6-0 at Ayresome Park in the third round, the Minnows of Hednesford Town 3-2 away in round two, Manchester City 1-0 at Maine Road in round five and Derby County 2-0 in the quarter-final at the Baseball Ground, 'Boro met Division Two side Chesterfield in the semi-final before almost 50,000 fans at Old Trafford.

The tie ended 3-3 after extra-time, 'Boro having been 2-0 down and then 3-2 up with just four minutes of the extra half-hour remaining.

A crowd of 30,339 saw 'Boro duly win the replay at Hillsborough 3-0 to qualify for the final, which, unfortunately, they lost 2-0 to Chelsea, for whom Roberto Di Matteo scored the quickest-ever goal at Wembley to get his side off to a flying start after just 42 seconds of play.

Five years later, 'Boro reached the last four for the second time without conceding a goal, only to lose 1-0 to Arsenal, again at Old

Trafford. En route to the semis they had ousted Wimbledon 2-0 (after a 0-0 draw), Manchester United 2-0, Blackburn Rovers 1-0 and Everton 3-0 (all three goals coming in seven minutes just before half-time). Then, in front of 61,168 fans in Manchester, an unfortunate own goal by Gianluca Festa gave the Gunners an undeserved victory, to the disappointment of everyone associated with Middlesbrough.

Moving on to 2006, and this time 'Boro, after eliminating Nuneaton Borough 5-2 in a replay following a hard-fought 1-1 draw at the non-League club's 6,000 capacity ground in Warwickshire, beat Coventry City 1-0 at home, also in a replay after a 1-1 scoreline. They accounted for Preston North End 2-0 at Deepdale and then defeated Charlton Athletic 4-2 in yet another replay after a 0-0 draw in London; they lost to West Ham United, for whom Marlon Harewood netted the winner in the 77th minute at Villa Park before 39,148 spectators.

FLYING WINGER

Billy Pease was a real speed merchant who spent seven years with 'Boro (1926–33), during which time he scored a record 102 goals as a winger in 238 appearances. Born in Leeds in 1898, he played for Leeds City and Northampton and served with the Royal Northumberland Fusiliers before joining 'Boro. One of the club's all-time greats, he was an outside-right, fast and clever, who netted 25 goals in the 1926/27 season, while centre-forward George Camsell bagged 63, a third of them made by wing wizard Pease.

CAUGHT ON CAMERA

Future Middlesbrough players Kevin Beattie and John Wark (when they were both registered with Ipswich Town) appeared together, along with Sylvester Stallone, Michael Caine, Bobby Moore, Pele, Ossie Ardiles and several other footballers, in the 1981 film *Escape To Victory*.

RECORD AGGREGATE WIN

The two-legged third round FA Cup tie between Middlesbrough and Leeds United in January 1946 produced a total of 17 goals. After a thrilling 4-4 draw at Elland Road, 'Boro turned on the style four days later to win the return game at Ayresome Park by 7-2, with Micky Fenton scoring a hat-trick. This gave 'Boro a club record 11-6 aggregate win.

This was the only season (1945/46) when all rounds of the FA Cup up to the semi-final stage were played over two legs.

ADVENTUROUS SMOKER

Jeremiah Dawson, Middlesbrough's goalkeeper in the 1880s, often smoked a pipe, sometimes during a match. He was also eccentric, and in one game against Ecclesfield, he decided to venture upfield in search of a goal, but his opposite number spotted him out of position, punted the ball 100 yards up to his outside-left who simply ran in to score unchallenged.

KEEP IT IN THE FAMILY

Over the years, there have been many family links with 'Boro. Here is a selection:

1. Mick Baxter's father Bill, played for Wolverhampton Wanderers and Aston Villa in the 1940s/early '50s.

2. Bob Baxter's son of the same name, starred for Darlington, Brighton & Hove Albion and Torquay United.

3. Mikkel Beck's father was a professional footballer in Denmark.

4. Bryan Robson and Gary Robson were both registered as players with West Bromwich Albion in 1981.

5. David Brown's father also kept goal for Manchester United and Hartlepool United.

6. George Burton's brother was a player with Cardiff City.

7. Middlesbrough goalkeeper Harry Harrison (1919–24) had two brothers who also occupied the number one position.

8   Ian Ironside kept goal for 'Boro in 1991/92. Some twenty-five years earlier his father Roy had stood between the posts for Rotherham United and Barnsley.

9   Joe Livingstone, who played centre-forward for 'Boro, Carlisle United and Hartlepool in the early 1960s, was the father of Steve, a striker with Chelsea, Grimsby Town, Coventry City and Blackburn Rovers (1986–98).

10 Bryan Orritt's son, Gareth, had unsuccessful trials with Middlesbrough as a teenager.

11 David Shearer, a 'Boro player from 1978 to 1983, is the brother of Duncan Shearer, who starred for Huddersfield Town, Blackburn Rovers and Swindon Town between 1982 and 1992. Neither, however, is related to Alan Shearer.

12 Brothers Billy and 'Sandy' Wardrobe were Middlesbrough players from 1899–1902 and 1910/11 respectively.

13 Cyril Knowles (Middlesbrough and Tottenham) is the brother of Peter Knowles (ex-Wolves).

14 Peter Donaghy's brother Ted was on 'Boro's books as a youth.

15 Bill Ellerington's son, also named Bill, played full-back for Southampton and England in the 1940s.

16 John McFarlane's brother, Hugh, played for Hibernian.

17 Billy Fox, from the club's early days of the 1880s, and his son, Vic Fox (1919–24), both played for Middlesbrough.

18   Uwe Fuchs's father, Fritz, was a professional footballer in Germany and later coach of HSV Hamburg.

19   Jim Gallagher (who played one game for 'Boro *v.* Manchester United in April 1921), was George Elliott's brother-in-law. Gallagher's son, Donald, played for 'Boro during the Second World War and was also a cricketer with Middlesbrough CC.

20   Bill Gates' brother, Eric, was a star player with Ipswich Town and also won an England cap.

21   John Hendrie is the nephew of Paul Hendrie, ex-Birmingham Citl's son, Lee, played for Aston Villa and several other clubs.

22   Tom Nibloe's son was briefly associated with Middlesbrough as an amateur.

23   Ronnie Dicks' younger brother, Alan, played for Chelsea, Southend United and Brighton & Hove Albion and later managed Bristol City.

24   David Mills' son was a youth team player with Middlesbrough in the 1990s, while Peter Creamer's son was initially on YTS forms with 'Boro.

25   Fabio da Silva Moriera is the cousin of 'Boro's Emerson Moises Costa.

26   Andy Todd's father, Colin, played for Sunderland, Nottingham Forest, Derby County, Birmingham City and England.

27   Middlesbrough star of the early 1900s, Jim Crawford, saw his daughter marry 'Boro' centre-forward Andy Wilson.

28   Marcus Bent's brother, Elliott, played for Dorchester Town, Welling United and Hampton & Richmond Borough.

29   It is unconfirmed, but I believe the Piercys, Frank and Bob, who both played at full-back for Middlesbrough in the 1890s, were related, possibly brothers.

THE CARR FAMILY

Four members of the Carr family from South Bank all played League football for Middlesbrough:

1. George, a centre-half or inside-forward, was born in January 1899 and scored 23 goals for 'Boro between 1919 and 1924. He also played for Bradford City, Leicester, City, Stockport County and Nuneaton Borough.

2. Harry, the eldest of the four brothers, was born in 1885. He played for South Bank in the 1910 Amateur Cup final defeat by Royal Marine Light Infantry and made one appearance for Sunderland before joining 'Boro in February 1911 as an amateur. He scored three goals in three League games as a centre-forward before leaving Ayresome Park. He represented England as an amateur.

3. Jacky is perhaps the most famous of the quartet. He was born in November 1891 and as a utility forward scored 81 goals in 449 first-class appearances for 'Boro, whom he served from December 1910 until May 1930, when he joined Blackpool. He also played for South Bank East End, South Bank and Hartlepools United (his last club). He retired in 1932 and died suddenly ten years later.

4. Willie, a centre-half, also played in the 1910 FA Amateur Cup final alongside his brother Harry. Born in 1888, he started out with his home town club before spending fourteen years with 'Boro, from April 1911 to May 1925, during which time he scored four goals in 118 senior matches. He died just ten months after Jacky.

5. Together, the four Carr brothers scored 111 goals in 640 League and Cup appearances for Middlesbrough over a period of twenty years from 1910. George, Jacky and Willie played together twenty-six times in 'Boro's first team.

RIVALS MIDDLESBROUGH IRONOPOLIS

Formed in 1889 by a handful of members of Middlesbrough FC, Middlesbrough Ironopolis (holding amateur status at the time) wanted the town to have a professional football club. Initially playing in the Northern League (1890–93), Ironopolis won three consecutive titles (with Middlesbrough second, second and fourth respectively) and in their first season reached the fourth qualifying round of the FA Cup, losing to Darlington. During the 1892/93 campaign, they made it through to the quarter-finals of the FA Cup before losing to Preston North End in a replay. Following an abortive attempt to enter the Football League in combination with neighbours Middlesbrough, Ironopolis was accepted into the Second Division for the 1839/94 season, following the resignation of Accrington. Competing in the League alongside the likes of Liverpool, Newcastle United and Woolwich Arsenal (now known simply as Arsenal), Ironopolis finished eleventh out of fifteen, recording impressive wins over Small Heath (now Birmingham City) by 3-0 and Ardwick (now Manchester City) by 2-0. Unfortunately, at the end of that season, the club lost its 32,000 capacity stadium, the Paradise Ground, which stood adjacent to Middlesbrough's Ayresome Park. Its financial position was poor, as gate receipts did not cover the cost of players' wages and travel to fixtures in distant parts of England. In February 1894, all of Ironopolis's professional players were served notice of the plans to liquidate the team. The club's final game was a 1-1 draw against South Bank on 30 April 1894. Ironopolis resigned from the Football League the following month and was immediately disbanded. Ironopolis and Bootle are the only two clubs to have spent a single season in the Football League. Middlesbrough ('The Scabs') played Ironopolis ('The Washers' or 'The Nops') six times in the Northern League between 1890 and 1893.

ANGLO-ITALIAN CUP

In May 1970, Middlesbrough entered the Anglo-Italian Cup for the first time, and although they remained unbeaten in their group, they failed to make the final.

Some twenty-three years later, in 1993/94, 'Boro again took part in this now defunct competition, and twelve months later they had another go. These are the results of 'Boro's games in the Anglo-Italian Cup:

1969/70

v. AS Roma	(h)	1-0
v. Lanerossi Vicenza	(h)	2-0
v. AS Roma	(a)	1-1
v. Lanerossi Vicenza	(a)	2-2

1993/94

v. Grimsby Town	(a)	1-2
v. Barnsley	(h)	3-1
v. Pisa	(a)	1-3
v. Ancona	(h)	0-0
v. Ascoli	(a)	0-3
v. Brescia Calico	(h)	0-1

1994/95

v. Piacenza	(h)	0-0
v. Cesena	(h)	1-1
v. Udinese	(a)	0-0
v. Ancona	(a)	1-3

Full Record

P	W	D	L	F	A
14	3	6	5	13	17

John Hickton top-scored with two goals in the 1969/70 tournament and John Hendrie, with three goals, was leading marksman in 1993/94. Both Jaime Moreno and Chris Morris netted in 1994/95.

WORLD CUP IN MIDDLESBROUGH

Three World Cup group games were played at Ayresome Park in July 1966. These were,

USSR 3 North Korea 0	Attendance 22,568
Chile 1 North Korea 1	Attendance 15,887
Italy 0 North Korea 1	Attendance 18,727

The last result was a shock and ended Italy's interest in the competition.

MIDDLESBROUGH BORN AND BRED

Over the course of time, several local-born players subsequently went on to join and serve Middlesbrough FC. Here is a good selection of local talent, who were all born and bred within reasonable striking distance of Breckon Hill, Linthorpe Road, Ayresome Park and the Riverside Stadium:

Nicky Agiadis, Harry Allport, Mick Angus, David Armstrong, Ian Bailey, Bill Barker, Fred Barker, Ray Barnard, Peter Beagrie, Bill Bell, Ian Bell, Stephen Bell, Walter Briggs, John Brown, Tom Brown, Tom E. Brown, Seth Buckley, Don Burluraux, George Burton, Sam Cail, Jim Callaghan, Andy Campbell, the Carr brothers (Billy, George, Harry and Jacky), Graeme Carter, Neville Chapman, Ernie Clark, Ben Cole, Andy Collett (Stockton-on-Tees), Harry Cook, Colin Cooper (from Sedgefield), Doug Cooper, Stephen Corden, Joe Crosier, Pat Cuff, John Curtis, Ben Davies, Billy Day, Francis Dowson, Stewart Downing, Curtis Edwards, Morris Emmerson, Andy Fletcher, Vic Fox, Jonathan Franks, Bill Gates, Joe Gettins, Jonathan Grounds, Jim Groves, Paul Hanford, Christian Hanson, George Hardwick, George Hawkins, George Hodgson, John Honeyman, Billy Horner, Ted Howling, Martin Hughes, John Johnson, Tom Jones, Chris Kamara, Gary Liddle, Joe Livingstone, Sam McClure, Garry MacDonald, Owen McGhee, Wilf Mannion, Nick Mohan, Alan Moody, Tony

Mowbray, David Murphy, Tom Murphy, Tom Murray, Ernie Muttit, 'Paddy' Nash, Ewan Lloyd, Paul Norton, Michael Oliver, Tony Ormerod, Cameron Parke, Gary Parkinson, Alan Peacock, Tony Peacock, Nick Peverill, Brian Phillips, Billy Pickstock, Bob Piercey, Frank Piercey, Jamie Pollock, Nathan Porritt, Malcolm Poskett, Bill Povey, Dick Pratt, Mark Proctor, Charlie Pugh, Andy Ramsay, Paul Richardson, Stan Rickaby, Connor Ripley, Stuart Ripley, Ben Roberts, Jack Roberts, Jim Robertson, John Robinson, Colin Ross, Sam Russell, Bill Scott, Harold Shepherdson, Maurice Short, Richard Smallwood, Alex Smith, Davey Smith, Gary Smith, Malcolm Smith, Ted Smith, Frank Spraggon, Phil Stamp, Robbie Stockdale, John Stone, Derek Stonehouse, Bob Stuart, Jim Suddick, Mark Summerbell, Andrew Swalwell, Andy Taylor, Brian Taylor, Mark Taylor, Jim Thackeray, Alex Thompson, Lee Tudor, Ted Verrill, Richard Ward, Bob Watson, Stan Webb, Luke Williams, 'Tiny' Williamson, Jonathan Woodgate, Billy Worrall, Charlie Wyke and Ernie Young.

And believe you me, there have been plenty more. Hopefully, in years to come, 'Boro will continually be blessed with local talent.

AMATEUR 'KEEPER

Ted Howling is the only amateur to keep goal for Middlesbrough in a major competitive match (League or Cup). Born in Stockton in 1885, he joined 'Boro in 1910 and stayed with the club for three years, during which time he made just one senior appearance, deputising for 'Tim' Williamson in a 1-0 home League defeat to Aston Villa in April 1911. He moved to Bristol City in 1913 and after the First World War assisted Bradford Park Avenue. Howling died in 1955, aged seventy.

SCOTS ON PARADE

Around 150 Scottish-born footballers have been associated with Middlesbrough since the club gained entry to the Football League in 1899. Here are some of them, listed from A–Z:

Bill Agnew, Andrew Aitken (also manager), George Aitken, Sam Aitken, Wally Auld, Bob Baxter, Simon Beaton, Chris Bennion, Billy Birrell, Jim Bissett, Harry Boardman, Kris Boyd, Alex Brown, John 'Jock' Brown, Jack Brownlie, Bobby Bruce, Hugh Caig, Ken Cameron, Alex Campbell, Joe Cassidy, Joe Clark, Alex Cochrane, Jimmy Cochrane, Eddie Connachan, Ron Coyle, Dave Cumming, Bob Currie, Andy Davidson, Bill Davidson, Ian Davidson, Stewart Davidson, Ian Dickson, Tom Doig, Peter Donaghy, John Dow, Bill Duguid, John Eckford, Bill Edwards, Willie Falconer, Charlie Ferguson, Willie Fernie, Bill Forrest, Paul Forrester, Alex Fraser, Hugh Good, Dan Gordon, Bob Gray, Andrew Halliday, Gary Hamilton, John Harkins, Joe Harris, George Henderson, John Hendrie, John Hewitt, John Hogg, Bob Hume, Jim Irvine, Andrew Jackson, Allan Johnson, Sam Lawrie, Alex Linwood, Billy McAllister, Tony McAndrew, Don McCallum, Jim McClelland, Bill Macaulay, Jim McClelland, Doug McCorquodale, Andy McCowie, Peter McCracken, Alex McCulloch, Bob McFarlane, John McFarlane, Andy McGuigan, Hugh McIlmoyle, John McKay, Peter McKennan, Duncan McKenzie, John McLean, Don McLeod, Stephen McManus, Don McPhail, Alex McRobbie, Alf Maitland, George Martin, Don Masson, Jim Mathieson, Jimmy Millar, Willie Millar, Lee Miller, Jackie Milne, Neil Mochan, Martin Moran, John Muir, Bobby Murdoch (also manager), Tom Nibloe, Jim Nicholl, Fergus Osborne, Jack Ostler, Jim Peggie, Bob Pender, George Reid, Alex Robertson, Bill Robertson, John Robinson, Barry Robson, Hector Shand, Bob Shannon, Tom Shaw, David Shearer, Bernie Slaven*, Jock Smith, John Smith, Graeme Souness, Bill Stage, John Stirling, Jim Tennant, Bobby Thomson, Ken Thomson, Kevin Thomson, Jimmy Townsend, Peter Turner, Archie Urquhart, Don Walker, Colin Walsh, Alex 'Sandy' Wardrobe, Billy Wardrobe, John Wark, Jim Watson, Jim Weir, Willie Whigham, Willie White, Derek Whyte, John Wilkie, Andy Wilson, Archie Wilson, David Winnie, Tommy Wright, Ray Yeoman, Ben Yorston and Bob Young.

*Slaven, although born in Paisley, went on to win seven caps for the Republic of Ireland.

Middlesbrough's other Scottish managers have been: Jimmy Howie, Peter McWilliam, Alex Mackie, Bruce Rioch and Gordon Strachan.

This reveals a strong international connection among players and managers with some top internationals in the list including Aitken (who won fourteen caps during his career), Boyd (18), Fernie (12), McManus (26), McWilliam (8), Marshall (7), Rioch (24), Robson (17), Souness (54), Stockdale (5), Strachan (50), Wark (29), Watson (6), Whyte (12) and Wilson (6). These fifteen players, as a group, gained a total of 288 full caps for their country.

Middlesbrough's most-capped Scottish players are Jock Marshall and Andy Wilson with six each.

ANGLO-SCOTTISH CUP WINNERS

Middlesbrough entered the short-lived Anglo-Scottish Cup competition twice in the mid-1970s and this proved to be a successful venture as the team won the trophy at the first time of asking.

After beating Sunderland 3-2 and Carlisle United 4-1 and drawing 2-2 with Newcastle United in the qualifying section of 1975/76, 'Boro made further progress by knocking out Aberdeen 4-2 on aggregate (2-0 and 2-2) in the quarter final and Mansfield Town 5-0 (3-0 and 2-0) in the two-legged semi-final, before taking on and beating Fulham 1-0 on aggregate in the final. The first game at Ayresome Park was attended by 14,700 fans and those present saw an own goal by Geoff Strong give 'Boro a victory. The return leg at Craven Cottage ended goalless in front of 13,723 fans.

Holders 'Boro went out in the group stage in 1976/77. After beating Hull City 2-0 (h) and Sheffield United 1-0 (a), they lost 3-0 at Newcastle and handed back the trophy.

Their full ASC record was,

P	W	D	L	F	A
12	9	2	1	25	7

John Hickton top-scored with five goals, followed by Graeme Souness with four, while David Armstrong, David Mills and Willey all netted three apiece. Armstrong, Stuart Boam, John Craggs and Mills played in all twelve games.

COCK OF THE NORTH

After beating and drawing with Sunderland (2-0 and 2-2) and twice defeating Newcastle United (3-2 and 4-3), Middlesbrough were crowned 'Cock of the North' champions after a mini tournament in October/November 1961.

FINED AND SUSPENDED

During the first part of the 1905/06 season, Middlesbrough fell foul of the FA, who fined the club a total of £250 and also suspended eleven of the twelve directors, including chairman R. W. Williams, for allegedly making irregular payments to players.

On 4 January 1906, the FA suspended the club because the £250 fine had not been paid. Thankfully, new chairman Lt-Col. T. Gibson Poole immediately sent a cheque to the appropriate department and all was well – for the time being!

BLACK CATS LINK

Over the past 125 years or so, more than fifty players have been associated with both Middlesbrough and Sunderland. Here, in alphabetical order, are most of those with a Black Cat connection

Bill Agnew, Stan Anderson, Julio Arca, Peter Beagrie, Harry Bell, Joe Blackett, Joe Bolton, Arthur Brown, John 'Jock' Brown, Mick Buckley, Geoff Butler, Harry Carr, Lee Cattermole, Brian Clough, Colin Cooper, Tom Craig, Johnny Crossan, Stan Cummins, John Curtis, Peter Davenport, Brian Deane, Andy Dibble, Stewart Downing, Bob Ferguson (1921), Bob Ferguson (reserve, 1936), Alan Foggon, Danny Graham, Dick Healey, David Hodgson, Justin Hoyte, Adam Johnson, Allan Johnson, Graham Kavanagh, John Kay, Matthew Kilgannon, George Kinnell, Grant Leadbitter, Jim Leslie, Peter McCracken, Jackie McMordie, Mark Proctor, Dicky Rooks, Gary Rowell, John Sphuler, goalkeeper Jim Stewart, Billy 'Rubber' Thompson, Joe Tomlin, Tommy

Urwin, Jim Watson, Owen Williams, Billy Worrall, Ben Yorston and 'Bolo' Zenden.

Sunderland players who guested for 'Boro during the Second World War were James Gorman, Albert Heywood (goalkeeper), Hugh McMahon, Jim Russell and John Sphuler, who later joined 'Boro.

Alex Mackie managed Sunderland (1899–1905) and Middlesbrough (1905/06) and Middlesbrough full-back George Hardwick also bossed Sunderland (1964/65), while former Sunderland inside-forward Raich Carter was manager of 'Boro (1963–66). Stan Anderson also served as 'Boro's manager (1966–73).

JAZZ FESTIVAL

In 1978, Ayresome Park hosted three days of music when the world-famous Newport Jazz Festival came to town. In a preview, the event was billed as the greatest gathering of jazz talent ever seen in Great Britain and was headlined by Ella Fitzgerald and Oscar Peterson. There were also performances by Buddy Rich, Lionel Hampton, Dizzy Gillespie and Art Blakey, to name just a few.

KEEPING UP APPEARANCES

Here are the leading appearance-makers for Middlesbrough. All substitute appearances are included in the respective totals.

Football League (Top 12)
1. 563 'Tim' Williamson
2. 462 Gordon Jones
3. 421 Jacky Carr
4. 418 George Camsell
5. 415 John Hickton
6. 409 John Craggs
7. 401 Jim Platt
8. 390 Dicky Robinson

9. 366 Mark Schwarzer
10. 360 Bill Harris
11. 359 David Armstrong
12. 348 Tony Mowbray

FA Cup (Top 15)

1. 40 Gordon Jones
2. 39 'Tim' Williamson
3. 37 John Hickton
4. 35 George Camsell
5. 34 Jim Platt
6. 33 John Craggs
7. 32 Mark Schwarzer
8. 30 Robbie Mustoe
9. 29 David Armstrong
10. 29 Stuart Boam
11. 29 Mick Fenton
12. 29 David Mills
13. 28 Jacky Carr
14. 28 Bill Gates
15. 26 Ronnie Robinson

Football League Cup (Top 15)

1. 47 Robbie Mustoe
2. 33 Colin Cooper
3. 33 Jim Platt
4. 32 Stephen Pears
5. 31 John Craggs
6. 30 John Hickton
7. 30 Tony Mowbray
8. 29 Steve Vickers
9. 28 David Armstrong
10. 28 Bernie Slaven
11. 27 Stuart Boam
12. 26 Curtis Fleming
13. 26 Gordon Jones
14. 26 Mark Schwarzer

15. 24   Willie Maddren

Others (including Europe; Top 10)

1. 28   Stephen Pears
2. 27   Bernie Slaven
3. 25   Colin Cooper
4. 24   Tony Mowbray
5. 23   Franck Queudrue
6. 21   Stuart Ripley
7. 21   Mark Schwarzer
8. 18   Stewart Downing
9. 17   John Hickton
10. 17   David Mills

All Competitions

1. 602   Tim Williamson
2. 532   Gordon Jones
3. 499   John Hickton
4. 488   John Craggs
5. 481   Jim Platt
6. 453   George Camsell
7. 449   Jacky Carr
8. 445   Mark Schwarzer
9. 431   David Armstrong
10. 425   Tony Mowbray
11. 424   Stephen Pears
12. 423   Colin Cooper
13. 416   Dicky Robinson

Facts

1. John Craggs made a club record 291 appearances in the 'old' First Division
2. Robbie Mustoe has played the most games for 'Boro in the Premiership (196). He has also appeared in more Cup games than any other 'Boro player, with an overall total of ninety – made up of thirty in the FA Cup, forty-seven in the League Cup and thirteen others.

RECORD WINS

Middlesbrough's biggest-ever win in a competitive match was 11-0, against Scarborough in an FA Cup qualifying round on 4 October 1890. 'Boro's goals that day were scored by Dennis (3), Johnston (3), Petrie (2), Allen, Stevenson and Wilson.

'Boro's best win in the Football League is 10-3 at Ayresome Park against Sheffield United on 18 November 1933. That afternoon a meagre crowd of just 6,461 saw George Camsell (4), Bobby Bruce (3), Bob Baxter, Charlie Ferguson and Fred Warren 'blunt' the Blades, and the visitors' woodwork was also struck twice.

To date, 'Boro's best League Cup wins is 7-0, against Hereford United (h) on 18 September 1996, when Fabrizio Ravanelli led the goal stampede with a four-timer.

EVER PRESENT

David Armstrong holds the record for most ever-present campaigns for Middlesbrough. He played in every League game seven seasons running from 1973/74 to 1979/80. Goalkeeper 'Tim' Williamson was an ever-present on five occasions between 1903 and 1921; Ray Yeoman had four 'full' seasons, 1959–63, and Stuart Boam was the mainstay of the defence for the duration of three campaigns: 1973/74, 1974/75 and 1976/77.

POINTING THE WAY

With the three points for a win rule having been in operation since 1973/74, Middlesbrough amassed a club record 94 points in season 1986/87 when they finished second in Division Three. The most the team had gained under the two points for a win rule was 65, when they won the Second Division title in 1973/74. They claimed 62 in 1926/27.

With the boot on the other foot, 'Boro's lowest points tally in a single League season is a meagre 22 (out of a possible 84) in 1923/24.

PROTEST UPHELD

After suffering a home 2-0 FA Cup qualifying round defeat at the hands of Middlesbrough in November 1890, Darlington protested the registration of 'Boro's left-half Billy Bell, alleging that he had played in a five-a-side game five months earlier in June, the day after he had actually signed as a professional for Middlesbrough. Bell, with the support by an affidavit signed by the match referee, claimed that the game had been played the week before his signing. Despite this, the protest was upheld and the tie was awarded to Darlington.

FIRST TOUR

Middlesbrough's first overseas European tour took them to Denmark in May 1907. They played two games in the Scandinavian country and won them both, beating a Danish University XI 5-3 and drawing 2-2 with a Danish Select XI in the space of twenty-four hours. Twelve months later, 'Boro returned to Denmark, where they beat a useful Danish Select XI 5-2, with Steve Bloomer scoring two of their goals.

QUICK OFF THE MARK

Tom Cochrane is on record for having scored the fastest 'Boro goal from the start of a game, netting against Manchester City after just six seconds in an emphatic 6-1 League win at Maine Road on 9 March 1938. Earlier in the season, 'Boro beat City, the reigning League champions, 4-0 at Ayresome Park, Cochrane again on target.

FAST RISERS

On 23 March 1974, Middlesbrough beat Oxford United 1-0 at Ayresome Park to clinch promotion to the First Division. It was the quickest elevation in Football League history as 'Boro still had five matches left to play. In the end, their winning margin over runners-up Luton Town was a massive 15 points.

HIGH SCORERS

The most goals scored by Middlesbrough in a complete League season was 122, accumulated in 1926/27 when they won the Second Division championship. Ten players between them scored those goals, with hot-shot George Camsell netting 59 of them. Billy Pease hit 23, Billy Birrell 16, Owen Williams nine, Jacky Carr 6, Jimmy McClelland 5 and Don Ashman, John McKay, Joe Williams and Herbert Smith (Port Vale) all scored 1 each.

'Boro netted 98 League goals in the 1930/31 season, bagged 93 in 1938/39, scored 92 in 1928/29 and notched 90 in 1959/60. In the latter season, 'Boro's 42 Second Division League games produced 154 goals, and there were some pretty high-scoring encounters, including 7-1, 6-2, 6-3, 5-1 and 5-2 wins over Derby County (a), Plymouth Argyle (h), Bristol City (h), Bristol Rovers (h) and Stoke City (a), 6-3, 5-0 and 5-2 defeats at Portsmouth, Leyton Orient and Lincoln City respectively, plus two thrilling 3-3 draws at Hull and at home to Liverpool. Brian Clough (with 39 goals) was 'Boro's top League scorer, followed by Alan Peacock with 13.

SAFE DRAW

Middlesbrough were not drawn against non-League opposition in the FA Cup for fifty-nine years between 1915 and 1974. They played and beat Goole Town 9-3 in a first-round tie on 9 January 1915 and had to wait until 3 January 1974 before meeting another team from outside the Football League. This was Grantham, who they beat 2-0 away, with David Mills and David Armstrong the scorers.

ONE-MATCH WONDERS

Since 1899/1900, when 'Boro first entered the Football League, well over fifty players have appeared in just one competitive game for the club. A handful actually stepped onto the field as a substitute for their one and only outing for the club, among them John Eustace, who saw just three minutes of action in the 1-1 draw with Liverpool in front of 42,247 fans at Anfield in February 2003. Paul Forrester's 'Boro career lasted for 25 minutes, coming for Phil Stamp halfway through the second-half of the 1-0 home defeat by Bolton in December 1993.

Midfielder Sean Kilgannon made one substitute appearance against Newcastle United in May 2000. Pat Lynch replaced David Mills for the last 30 minutes of 'Boro's 1-0 League defeat at QPR in March 1972 Malcolm Poskett managed only 12 minutes of action as a 'Boro player, coming on against Hull City at Ayresome Park in October 1973 and Tom Craddock, a prolific goalscorer at both junior and reserve team levels, was given a run out as a substitute against Fulham at Craven Cottage in May 2006.

Although he played for only the last 9 minutes, Craddock was part of both club and Premiership history, being one of sixteen Englishmen named by 'Boro boss Steve McClaren that afternoon.

Neil Illman played 17 minutes of League football for 'Boro, after coming on as a 73rd minute substitute in the 1-0 home defeat by Bristol City on 6 November 1993.

Full-back Stephen Corden, son of Middlesbrough director Dick Corden, made his senior debut for the club in a Second Division game at Wimbledon's Plough Lane in August 1985. Unfortunately, young Stephen, aged eighteen at the time, fractured his leg in the tenth minute of a 3-0 defeat and never played competitive football again.

Young Ted Marcroft scored in his only game for 'Boro in a 1-1 First Division draw at Sheffield Wednesday in January 1932.

Jimmy Suddick scored on his only appearance for 'Boro in a 1-1 League draw at Sunderland in January 1904.

Here are a few more of 'Boro's one-match wonders:

Bob Anderson (1947), Fred Barker (1906), Bill Bell (1899), Colin Blackburn (1980), Harry Boddington (1903), Ray Bryan (1936), Seth

Buckley (1899), Hugh Caig (1914), Frank Chipperfield (1919), Ernie Clark (1899), Joe Clark (1899), Ed Coleman (1975), Joe Davison (1919), Tom Featherstone (1903), Bill Flint (1909), Jack French (1924), Connor Gallacher (1946), Jim Gallagher (1920), Daniel Gordon (1908), Ted Hanlon (1906), Albert Hassell (1907), John Hastie (1920), Harry Hawkins (1935), John Honeyman (1919), Ted Howling (1910), Jim Maddison (1946), Andrew McGuigan (1902), Alan McRobbie (1911), Fabio Moriera (1997), Alan Nobbs (1980), Tom Paterson (1974), Ron Patterson (1951), Fred Priest (1906), Jack Roberts (1906), John Robinson (1919), John Smith (1933), James Stott (1899), John Surtees (1931), Otto Trechman (1905), George Wardle (1937), Fred Wilson (1967), David Winnie (1994), William Worrall (1905) and Ernie Young (1920).

AMATEUR TOP DOGS

Middlesbrough won the FA Amateur Cup twice in the 1890s. In the 1894/95 season, after eliminating Bishop Auckland 3-2, Darlington (2-0 in a second replay after two 1-1 draws), Old Brightonians 8-0 and the King's Own Royal Lancashire Regiment (from Portsmouth) 4-0 in the semi-final at Derby, 'Boro took on the holders Old Carthusians (a team made up of Charterhouse school old boys) in the final at the Headingley Stadium where, in front of 4,000 spectators, they won 2-1 with goals from Dave Mullen and Arthur 'Happy' Nelmes.

Three years later, in 1897/98, 'Boro lifted the trophy for a second time, defeating Uxbridge 2-0 in the final at Crystal Palace with goals by Bishop and Kemplay before an estimated crowd of 8,000. After knocking out Leadgate Park 4-0, Thornaby Utopians 3-2 (following a 1-1 draw) and Casuals (London) 1-0, 'Boro beat Thornaby 2-1 in the semi-final, played behind closed doors at the Brotton ground in the Cleveland hills. This game, in fact, was scheduled to take place at Darlington, but due to a smallpox epidemic, the FA switched the game to Brotton.

TOO MUCH FREIGHT

In the 1986/87 season, Middlesbrough beat Doncaster Rovers 3-0, lost 2-1 at Chesterfield, defeated Halifax Town 2-1 at The Shay and knocked out Rochdale on penalties to reach the semi-final of the Freight Rover Trophy. Unfortunately, they went no further in the competition, losing 1-0 at home to Mansfield Town.

'Boro's record in the FRT was,

P	W	D	L	F	A
5	3	0	2	10	7

Paul Proudlock and Archie Stephens top-scored, each netting two goals.

FIRST TROPHY: THE CLEVELAND CHALLENGE CUP

In March 1882, Middlesbrough lifted their first ever trophy, defeating Redcar in the final of the Cleveland Association Challenge Cup at Saltburn before a crowd of 1,000. 'Boro then won the next three finals of this same competition, all against Redcar, and in 1886 the teams met again in the final for a fifth successive time.

In front of 5,000 spectators, again the Saltburn ground, the two rivals played out a hard-fought goalless draw after extra-time, although the game itself was brought to an end just short of the 120-minute mark after the Redcar defender Dick Paul broke his leg.

The replay, staged at Redcar, was a rather one-sided contest as 'Boro raced to an 8-1 win against the team, missing two of its key players, plus the unlucky Paul.

All teams that enter any Football Association competition such as the FA Cup, the FA Trophy or the FA Vase must enter the Cleveland Association Cup, know officially known as the Senior Cup, the name change taking place in 1902 when Middlesbrough were the first winners. 'Boro, in fact, have won the competition no less than fifty two times, which is the most by any team, their last success being in 2012.

GYPSY'S CURSE

Many 'Boro' supporters, male and female, young and old, have heard of the legend about a group of gypsies who placed a curse on Ayresome Park after they were removed from the site, which restricted 'Boro' from winning a major trophy while they were in residence. But there is also the tale of the Ayresome Park ground being haunted by a young spirit called Ned, who would appear at the gates of Ayresome Park if 'Boro were going to win. As it was, 'Boro never won a major trophy between 1898 and 2004!

A ROUND DOZEN

There haven't been many matches in the history of football that have produced a 6-6 scoreline. 'Boro, however, have been involved in two twelve-goal thrillers. Besides drawing 6-6 with Charlton in a League game in 1960, they also shared six goals with Hibernian at East Road in a friendly in November 1959. A crowd of 15,000 saw Alan Peacock (2), Willie Fernie (2), Brian Clough and Bill Harris score for 'Boro.

INTER-LEAGUE GAMES ON 'BORO SOIL

Four Inter-League games took place at Ayresome Park:

17 February 1912	Football League 2 Scottish League 0	Attendance 24,149
22 March 1950	Football League 3 Scottish League 1	Attendance 39,352
20 March 1968	Football League 2 Scottish League 0	Attendance 34,190
15 March 1972	Football League 3 Scottish League 2	Attendance 19,996

SEMI-FINAL DISAPPOINTMENT

Manchester City knocked Middlesbrough out of the 1975/76 League Cup in the semi-final. After eliminating Bury (2-1), Derby County (1-0), Peterborough United 3-0 and Burnley 2-0, 'Boro succumbed 4-1 on aggregate to City over two legs, winning 1-0 at home but losing 4-0 away. A decade later, after beating Carlisle United 2-0 at Ayresome Park (in front of just 2,177 spectators), Middlesbrough were knocked out of the Full Members Cup in the Northern Area semi-final in November 1985, beaten by Hull City, who won 3-1 after extra-time at Boothferry Park when the attendance was 3,657. In 1991/92, 'Boro went out of the League Cup at the semi-final stage again, beaten this time by the other Manchester club, United, who won 2-1 on aggregate (0-0 at Ayresome Park, 2-1 at Old Trafford). On their way to the last four, 'Boro had defeated Bournemouth (3-2 over two legs), Barnsley 1-0, Manchester City 2-1 and Peterborough United 1-0 in a replay after a 0-0 draw.

ZENITH DATA SYSTEMS CUP

Middlesbrough played in this competition three seasons running from 1989–92, reaching the final in 1990, only to lose 1-0 to Chelsea in front of 76,369 fans at Wembley. This is 'Boro's full ZDSC record:

1989/90

Round 2	*v.* Port Vale	(h)	3-1
Round 3	*v.* Sheffield Wednesday	(a)	4-1
Area s/final	*v.* Newcastle Utd	(h)	1-0
Area final (1)	*v.* Aston Villa	(a)	2-1
Area final (2)	*v.* Aston Villa	(h)	2-1
Full Final	*v.* Chelsea	(n)	0-1

1990/91

Round 1	*v.* Hull City	(h)	3-1
Round 2	*v.* Manchester City	(a)	1-2

1991/92

Round 2	*v.* Derby County	(h)	4-2
Round 3	*v.* Tranmere Rovers	(h)	0-1

P	W	D	L	F	A
10	7	0	3	20	11

Striker Bernie Slaven scored nine of 'Boro's twenty ZDSC goals, including a hat-trick in the 4-1 win over Sheffield Wednesday in December 1989, when a crowd of 8,716 fans assembled at Ayresome Park. An attendance of almost 17,000 saw Colin Cooper net the second-half winner in the 'derby' win over Newcastle United in the quarter-final tie at Ayresome Park in January 1990. The official turnouts for the two semi-finals in January/February 1990 were 16,547 at Villa Park and 20,806 at Ayresome Park, the latter being the biggest of that season's competition other than for the final.

FABULOUS FABRIZIO

Fabrizio Ravanelli scored 32 goals in 50 first-class appearances for Middlesbrough during the 1996/97 season. The Italian, signed from Juventus, netted 25 of his goals in 25 games at the Riverside Stadium, including a debut hat-trick against Liverpool. He also became the first player to score a goal for 'Boro at Wembley Stadium, doing so against Leicester City in the 95th minute of the 1997 League Cup final which ended 1-1. After scoring, he raced away to celebrate with his trademark 'shirt over the head' routine.

BIG LOSS

In March 2014, Middlesbrough chairman Steve Gibson made public the club's financial situation, revealing a loss of just under £14 million and a wage bill of more than £36 million, which covered an eighteen-month period. It meant that Gibson had continued his multi-million pound support for the club through his 75 per cent holding via the parent company Gibson O'Neill, and pledged to carry on doing so for at least another twelve months. The club's directors also stated that, due to lower gate receipts and two third-round knockouts in the FA Cup, there had been a considerable' reduction in the amount of money coming in. Income alone from Cup competitions fell dramatically from £1.8 million to £207,000 and, with a hefty wage bill, the battle to restructure the operation is ongoing. In fact, 'Boro's wage bill went up from £27 to 704 million the previous year, but for a shorter twelve-month period up to 31 December 2009, Gibson's depth of commitment to the club is plain to see, with external debts of £27.8 million being refinanced by Gibson O'Neill and replaced with a huge internal debt, indicating clearly the chairman's strategy of keeping a tight control of the finances with the £13.8 million loss compared to a £63,000 profit last time.

MEMBERSHIP OF THE FOOTBALL LEAGUE

After raising £1,000 from the sale of £1 shares, Middlesbrough applied to join the Football League in May 1899. Backed by North East neighbours Newcastle United and Sunderland, as well as by Harry Walker, the North Riding's FA representative on the FA Council, the club's application was heard at a meeting held at The Old Boar's Head Hotel, Manchester. Nine clubs in total wanted to play in the Second Division for the 1899/1900 season; 'Boro were one of them and they were successful with their application, receiving seventeen votes, two more than Blackpool, who were seeking re-election, but eleven fewer than Loughborough (re-elected). Chesterfield also got elected with twenty-seven votes.

CLOSE SHAVE

Middlesbrough almost came a cropper when they met non-League side Bishop's Stortford in a third-round FA Cup tie at Ayresome Park in January 1983. The underdogs were two-nil down at half-time, Stephen Bell having bagged both for 'Boro, but Richard Bradford netted twice in the second half to earn Bishop's a replay. Then, in front of 6,000 fans at the George Wilson Stadium, 'Boro trailed 1-0 to a 'Kipper' Lynch goal before Duncan Shearer saved their blushes with a brace after the interval.

FIRST LEAGUE DEFEAT

Unfortunately, Middlesbrough's first-ever Football League game ended in a 3-0 Second Division defeat away at Lincoln City on 2 September 1899. A crowd of 2,000 saw this team in action: E. Smith; T. Shaw, A. Ramsey; H. Allport, J. McNally, J. McCracken; R. Wanless, G. Longstaffe, J. Gettins, R. Page and C. Pugh.

MAKING A POINT

After losing their first three Second Division matches against Lincoln City and Port Vale away and Small Heath at home, Middlesbrough gained their first Football League point with a 1-1 draw away to New Brighton on 16 September 1899.

NO JOY IN SIMOD CUP

Middlesbrough competed in the Simod Cup in successive seasons of 1987/88 and 1988/89. In the former, they were eliminated in the first round by Ipswich Town 1-0 at Portman Road while in 1977/88, after beating Oldham Athletic 1-0, Portsmouth 2-1 (after extra-time) and Coventry City 1-0, they went out of the competition by losing 3-2 at home to Crystal Palace in front of 16,314 spectators.

PAGE BOY

Middlesbrough's first goal in the Football League was scored by Robert Page in a 3-1 defeat at Port Vale on 4 September 1899. Page netted one more League goal during the season, in a 5-2 home win over New Brighton in mid-January.

MONEY LOAN

In April 1986, hard-up 'Boro had to borrow £30,000 from the Professional Footballers' Association to pay the players' wages.

INTO THE LEAGUE

Under manager John Robson, Middlesbrough finished fourteenth (out of eighteen) at the end of their first season in the Football League. This was their full record in the Second Division in 1899/1900:

Venue	P	W	D	L	F	A	Points
Home	17	8	4	5	28	15	20
Away	17	0	4	13	11	54	4
Total	34	8	8	18	39	69	24

'Boro's biggest win was 8-1 *v.* Burton Swifts (h) on 11 November, while their heaviest defeat was 7-1 at Chesterfield in late January. Jim McCracken made most appearances (33); he missed the 6-1 win at Small Heath six days into 1900. Harry Allport played in 31 games, Charlie Pugh (31) and Andrew Ramsey (27) and the top goalscorers were Pugh (with 7), Tom Lamb (6) and George Reid and Joe Murphy (5 each). 'Boro's best home attendance was 10,000 *v.* Small Heath on 9 September; their lowest 3,000 *v.* Loughborough Town in December. And barely 500 spectators witnessed the away game at Loughborough in mid-April. Middlesbrough's average home League attendance in their first season was 5,271.

CLEVELAND CUP WINNERS

Starting in 1881/82, Middlesbrough won four Cleveland Cup finals on the trot, all against neighbours Redcar, before making it a nap-hand with a rousing 8-1 replay win over the same opponents in April 1886. A crowd of 5,000 at the Saltburn ground had witnessed an initial 0-0 draw after extra-time, before 'Boro went goal crazy in the replay.

OILED BY MAGPIES

Unfortunately, Middlesbrough failed to qualify from their North East group of the 1974/75 Texaco Cup competition, winning only one of their three games, 1-0 at Sunderland with a David Armstrong goal. They lost by the same score at home to Carlisle United and suffered a humiliating 4-0 defeat at the hands of Newcastle United at St James' Park.

NORTHERN LEAGUE RECORDS

As founder members, Middlesbrough went on to compete in the Northern League for ten seasons before joining the Football League Division Two for the 1899/1900 season. They played a total of 184 games in the NL, winning ninety-one, drawing twenty-eight and losing thirty-five, scoring 369 goals and conceding 203. They won the title three times (1893/94, 1894/95 and 1896/97), finished runners-up on three occasions (1890/91, 1891/92 and 1897/98), and came third twice (1895/96 and 1898/99).

LONG TRIP

In May 1975, Middlesbrough enjoyed a month down under, playing some 9,500 miles away from the UK, on tour to Australia and New Zealand. They fulfilled seven matches in total, of which five were won and two drawn. After sharing the spoils with Western Australia and South Australia (both games ending level at 1-1), 'Boro went goal crazy, battering Queensland 4-0, Balgownie 5-3, Northern New South Wales 8-0, Auckland 5-1 in New Zealand and a Tahiti Select XI 6-0. Of the 30 goals scored, David Mills netted ten and Harry Charlton and Bobby Murdoch four each. The latter's tally included a hat-trick (two penalties) against Northern NSW.

FESTIVAL WOE

To celebrate the Festival of Britain, Middlesbrough played a friendly against the Yugoslavian side Partizan Belgrade on 12 May 1951 and in front of 20,000 spectators were beaten 3-2.

TESTIMONIALS

Over the course of time, Middlesbrough have played in a number of testimonial/benefit matches for ex-players, other personnel and various charities, and here are some of the more interesting contests, with the name of the beneficiary in brackets:

27 April 1931	Hearts 1 'Boro 5 (Bill Murray)
17 October 1935	Newcastle United 3 'Boro 2 (Gresford Colliery Fund)
20 August 1938	Sunderland 4 'Boro 2 (FA Jubilee Fund)
11 November 1969	'Boro 4 All Stars XI 3 (Gordon Jones)
7 May 1973	'Boro 7 England XI 5 (Harold Shepherdson)*
26 March 1974	Darlington 0 'Boro 4 (Alan Sproates)
7 May 1974	'Boro 4 Leeds United 4 (Billy Gates)
10 May 1974	Newcastle United 5 'Boro 3 (Tony Green)+
28 October 1975	'Boro 2 Dinamo Zagreb 2 (Frank Spraggon)
19 April 1977	'Boro 6 Sunderland 1 (John Hickton)°
9 May 1978	'Boro 5 Scottish XI 5 (Willie Maddren)
1 October 1980	'Boro 1 Middlesbrough XI 1 (David Armstrong)
20 May 1982	Cliftonville 2 'Boro 2 (John Platt)

16 November 1982	'Boro 3 Newcastle United 3 (John Craggs)
17 May 1983	'Boro 1 England XI 2 (George Hardwick/ Wilf Mannion)
28 April 1986	'Boro 2 Newcastle United 1 (David Mills)

*A crowd of 10,674 attended this game for England's World Cup-winning trainer.

+ An exceptional crowd of 27,938 saw this eight-goal encounter at St James' Park.

º Hickton scored a hat-trick in his own testimonial in front of 10,500 fans.

GOALS GALORE

A total of 52 goals were scored in the nine friendly matches played by Middlesbrough in 1939/40. In this sequence, 'Boro beat Hartlepool United 5-4, Stockton 6-3, Darlington 5-1, Barnsley 4-2 and Newcastle United 5-2. Mick Fenton netted 18 of 'Boro's, goals including a four-timer against Barnsley in December.

IRISH EYES ARE SMILING, FOR 'BORO

Middlesbrough won all four games on tour in Ireland in May 1952. They beat Glentoran 3-0, Glenavon 3-0, Cork 5-1 and Drumcondra 6-1. Lindy Delaphena scored in all four games (5 goals in total).

CORONATION CRACKER

To celebrate the Coronation of Queen Elizabeth II, Middlesbrough and Sunderland played a friendly at Roker Park on 6 May 1953. A crowd of 5,896 saw 'Boro win 4-3 with goals from Arthur Fitzsimons (2), Geoff Walker and Bill Edwards.

LIVE ON TELEVISION

Middlesbrough first appeared live on television on 16 March 1954 when the second-half of their floodlit friendly against Falkirk at Brockville Park was shown live on the BBC. The Scottish club won the game 2-1.

DUTCH COURAGE

Middlesbrough played in Holland for the first time in May 1953. They contested two games, drawing 2-2 with a strong Dutch XI and beating the Dutch National Reserve team 3-1. 'Boro drew 3-3 with PSV Eindhoven at Ayresome Park in March 1958, and ten years later they were beaten at home by Go Ahead Deventer. Other games against Dutch opposition include a 2-0 win in Leeuwarden, a 3-0 home victory over SC Cambuur, a 4-0 drubbing of Groningen at Ayresome Park (1972) and an impressive 1-0 home win over Ajax Amsterdam (1978).

NORTH AMERICAN TOUR

In 1987/88, Middlesbrough played four games on tour in North America. They beat San Jose Earthquakes 2-1 and Calgary Kickers 2-0, lost 2-1 to Seattle Storm and drew 1-1 with Albany Capitals. Seattle Storm had earlier lost 2-1 in a friendly at Ayresome Park and in August 1988, they were beaten again on 'Boro soil, this time 3-0.

EARLY BATH!

Jimmy Watson had the misfortune to be the first Middlesbrough player to get sent off in a major competition. He took an early bath during the FA Cup tie against Preston North End in January 1909. The first 'Boro player dismissed in a League game was Andy Wilson, sent packing against Liverpool in March 1915. And in the League Cup, 'Boro's first sending off was Bobby Thomson at Plymouth in October 1981. Over a period of almost ten years (between April 1980 and January 1989), no less than twenty-three Middlesbrough players were dismissed in League and Cup games. John Hickton and Eric McMordie were both sent off in 'Boro's 2-0 League win at Norwich in August 1968. Tony Mowbray and David Currie took early baths in 'Boro's 1-0 defeat at Derby in November 1983 and Gary Hamilton and Peter Beagrie both saw red in 'Boro's 2-0 last game of the season win at Shrewsbury in May 1985. 'Boro had defender Gary Pallister dismissed in a 2-1 defeat at Shrewsbury on the last day of the 1985/86 season, which saw them relegated to the Third Division. When Middlesbrough beat Sunderland 6-0 in front of almost 30,000 fans at Ayresome Park in a League game in March 1936, two visiting players were sent off: inside-right Raich Carter (later to manage 'Boro) and his wing-partner Bert Davis. A similar thing happened in March 1974 when Sunderland again had two players dismissed – Dennis Tueart and Bobby Kerr – in 'Boro's 2-0 League win.

OFF AGAIN!

Many professional footballers pride themselves on a clean disciplinary record, and would take any sending off to heart. But when midfielder Lee Cattermole, who played in sixty-nine League games for Middlesbrough (2005–08) trudged off the pitch against Hull City at the KC Stadium in November 2013, without even looking at what card the referee was showing him, this told you that it was a man who had been there before! In fact, Cattermole, at the tender age of twenty-five, had, there and then, the second highest amount of red cards in Premier League history, with seven. At the time, Cattermole (referred to as some as Clattermole) averaged a sending off every twenty-six games.

FIRST OFF THE BENCH

Substitutes were first allowed in Football League games in the 1965/66 season, and the first player to be named as 'Boro's No. 12 was inside-forward Bryan Orritt against Manchester City (home) on 21 August of that season. The Welshman wasn't called into action, but he was introduced by manager Raich Carter as a second-half substitute in place of right-back Neville Chapman in the away fixture against Preston North End on 11 September 1965 to become the club's first used substitute. 'Boro drew the game 1-1. Orritt was also the first 'sub' used by 'Boro in a home League game; he came on when goalkeeper Bob Appleby was injured against Charlton Athletic a week later.

AND FINALLY, A GENERAL LOOK AT MIDDLESBROUGH

M   Managers... thirty-five have been in office since 1899.

I   Ironopolis... 'Boro's local neighbours and rivals from yesteryear.

D   Draw... a League record 6-6 with Charlton Athletic in 1960.

D   Derbies... several against Newcastle United and Sunderland.

L   League Champions... Division One in season 1994/95.

E   Ever-present... David Armstrong from 1972 to 1980.

S   Strikers... Bloomer, Camsell, Clough, Elliott, Hickton, Slaven, etc.

B   'Boro... Middlesbrough's officially adopted nickname.

R   Riverside Stadium... home ground, opened in 1995.

O   Oldest debutant for club... Viv Anderson, aged thirity-eight in 1995.

U   UEFA Cup... runners-up in 2006, beaten 4-0 in final by Sevilla.

G   Goalkeeper... Tim Williamson, record 602 appearances: 1901–23

H   Hardwick... George, left-back, captain of 'Boro and England.

F   Formation of the club... season 1876/77

O   Orritt...'Boro's first substitute in 1965.

O   One line... club contact

T   Ten-three win over Sheffield United in 1933.

B   Best Home Crowd... 53,802 *v.* Newcastle, 1949.

A   Amateur Cup Winners... twice in the 1890s.

L   Lincoln City... 'Boro's first League opponents.

L   League membership... gained in 1899.

C   Champions of League Division 2... 1973/74

L   League Cup winners, 2004 (*v.* Bolton)

U   Unbeaten in 24 League games... 1973 and 1974.

B   Best football club in Middlesbrough... 'Boro!

BIBLIOGRAPHY

Eleven contributors, *The Who's Who of Middlesbrough* (Breedon Books, 2007)

Glesper, Harry, *Middlesbrough: The Complete Record: 1876–1989* (Breedon Books, 1989).

Golesworthy, Maurice, *We Are The Champions* (Pelham Books, 1972).

Hugman, Barry J., *The PFA Footballers' Who's Who/Fact File* (Lennard/Queene Anne Press/Mainstream Publishing, 1995–2012).

Hugman, Barry J., *The PFA, Premier & Football League Players' Records: 1946–1998* (Queen Anne Press, 1998)

Joyce, Michael, *Football League Players' Records: 1888 to 1939* (SoccerData Publication, 2002)

Mourant, Andrew, Rollin, Jack, *The Essential History of England* (Headline Publishing, 2002)

Rothmans/Sky Sports Yearbooks (Queen Anne Press/Headline Publishing, 1970–2014)

FA Football Yearbooks (various editions from 1958)

Middlesbrough FC's official matchday programmes (various, 1950 to date)

Charles Buchan's Football Monthly (various issues, 1954 to 1974)

FourFourTwo football magazine (various editions from 1990)

Official website of Middlesbrough AFC

Footballzz.co.uk

www.Statto.com

www.11v11.com

Vitalfootball.co.uk

Tony Matthews, author.

ALSO AVAILABLE FROM AMBERLEY PUBLISHING

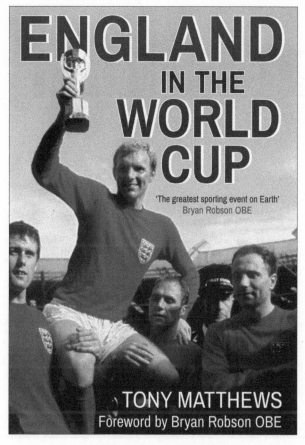

England in the World Cup

Tony Matthews

Tony Matthews explores each of England's World Cup appearances, from Brazil 1950 to Brazil 2014, giving detailed match reports and stats along with a historical narrative to set each tournament in its context. This is essential reading for any fan of the beautiful game.

978 1 4456 1948 4

160 pages

Available from all good bookshops or order direct from our website www.amberleybooks.com

ALSO AVAILABLE FROM AMBERLEY PUBLISHING

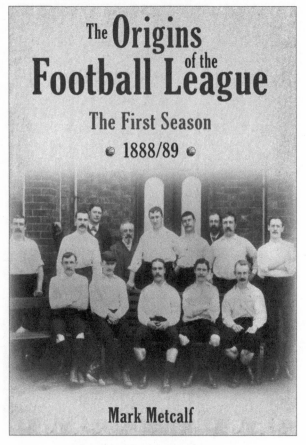

The **Origins** of the **Football League**

The First Season

1888/89

Mark Metcalf

Origins of the Football League
Mark Metcalf

For the first time, this history of the Football League season 1889/89
is told in great depth, with reports on every match and profiles of all
those who played.

978 1 4456 1881 4
224 pages

Available from all good bookshops or order direct
from our website www.amberleybooks.com